Spirituality in the Selfie
Culture of Instagram

Spirituality in the Selfie Culture of Instagram

PETRA P. SEBEK

WIPF & STOCK · Eugene, Oregon

SPIRITUALITY IN THE SELFIE CULTURE OF INSTAGRAM

Copyright © 2019 Petra P. Sebek. All rights reserved. Except for brief quotations in critical publications or reviews, no part of this book may be reproduced in any manner without prior written permission from the publisher. Write: Permissions, Wipf and Stock Publishers, 199 W. 8th Ave., Suite 3, Eugene, OR 97401.

Wipf & Stock
An Imprint of Wipf and Stock Publishers
199 W. 8th Ave., Suite 3
Eugene, OR 97401

www.wipfandstock.com

PAPERBACK ISBN: 978-1-5326-7316-0
HARDCOVER ISBN: 978-1-5326-7317-7
EBOOK ISBN: 978-1-5326-7318-4

Manufactured in the U.S.A.   FEBRUARY 6, 2019

Graphs from: www.hashtracking.com

Contents

Acknowledgements | vii
Introduction | ix

1 Defining Cyberspirituality | 1
2 Spirituality and Selfie Culture | 19
3 Spirituality on Instagram | 32
4 Future Challenges for Cyberspirituality | 78

Glossary | 87
Bibliography | 91

Acknowledgements

This book is a result of taking a journey of studying for an MA in Applied Spirituality, organized by Spirituality Institute for Research and Education and Waterford Institute of Technology in Ireland.

I would like to express my gratitude to Dr. Michael O' Sullivan, Program Director, for the encouragement and opportunity to participate in the program. The expertise, support, and enthusiasm of Dr. Bernadette Flannagan, Director of Research, made this project a very enriching and joyful experience.

I also wish to give praise to all the lecturers: Anne Marie Dixon, Amanda Dillon, Jack Finnegan, Brian Dooney, David Halpin, Noelia Molina, Mike Serrage, Bernadette Masterson, and Niamh Brennan. You have been a true inspiration. Many thanks to Fergus Lyons, principal of St. Mary's school in Sandyford, for his help.

My MA journey would be a very different experience without all my classmates. I hope that I managed to persuade you that hugs are very important.

Special thanks to my spiritual director Pat Coyle who was the best companion one could wish for. I hope to continue dancing with her occasionally.

Acknowledgements

My mother Dragica and my mother-in-law Anka are my biggest cheerleaders back in Croatia.

My family: husband Tomi and our sons Martin and Benjamin—you are my everything.

Introduction

WHEN WE THINK OF stories, we often think of favorite books or movies, or maybe sometimes we recall a memory of our parents talking to us before our bedtime. These are samples of traditional storytelling. Storytelling today is mainly visual, happening on the Internet and being shared on social media. Visual storytelling describes the process of telling a story without the need for lines of text or audio. Some images can tell an entire story and open completely new worlds. The expression that "a picture paints a thousand words" is even more powerful in the world of social media today.

Some people express negative attitude about social networks saying that they only emphasize superficial (sometimes even false) self-expressions. This may be true for some users, and it is the reason why the term "selfie culture" is emerging. Without doubt we can see negative aspects and effects that social media can have on individuals and societies. But is that all? Could they also be a world for inspiration, connection, communication, and uplifting others? Is there spirituality in the selfie culture?

One must be aware that for many people, especially young ones, social networks are public places in which they create their digital identities and build communities,

Introduction

and they express their daily struggles but also their daily inspirations. In the past few decades, the Internet has become the essential part of everyday life for many individuals. The border between offline and online life has become fluid, and building one's digital identity has become an inseparable part of building one's identity in general. With smartphones and social media becoming a part of our life, we never switch off anymore and we are trying to incorporate our interests and values as a part of our digital identity. Digital technology has become an important platform for extending and altering religious and spiritual practice for many people. Some are seeking to join virtual counterparts of their offline spiritual communities, and some are using the Internet as an open field to search for and communicate with similar-minded individuals and to form completely new communities online.

My professional background is in the media—I was working as a journalist and producer for Croatian radio television for more than 15 years, with religion being my area of coverage for most of that time. With the development of digital news platforms, I transferred to work in the digital newsroom and deepened my knowledge about social media channels. Now, being an MA student of Applied Spirituality, I would like to bring together my experience from both the spiritual and the digital world. Embarking on a spiritual path made me understand that spirituality cannot be separated from other parts of our lives. Spirituality must come from within, from life, from concrete circumstances and injustices which call you to find your inner calling, your vocation, and your meaning of life. During my MA one of the most important words was *authenticity*. Learning and reflecting about it has had a transformative effect on my

Introduction

personal inner life and encouraged me to look for examples of how other people communicate about it.

I am a daily user of social media apps, and I noticed that when I wish to express my feelings about spiritual moments, I tend to do that through visual storytelling by taking photographs, rather than journaling or writing in general. And when I do that, I tend to use Instagram as a platform for sharing. This fact motivated me to choose Instagram for this study and to try to find out how others are using it. I hope that this research will help to understand how people use Instagram to search for, share, listen to, observe, and witness their spirituality.

Instagram is a social media network based on the sharing of images. It effectively works only by using the application on mobile devices and the images shared there are mainly taken with the mobile device itself—"instantly." It was launched in 2010. Registered users can upload videos and photos to the network through the application, apply digital filters while doing so, use hashtags with their posts in order to link them to certain topics, themes, or trends, and add locations through geotags. It is an only-image based social network. There is a difference between only-image based social media platforms and text-based ones. The image-based social networks communicate a more personal experience, so they can show us how spirituality is lived, in what settings, and relations. Instagram rapidly gained popularity and was acquired by Facebook in 2012. Instagram is an increasingly popular social network, with 800 million active global users at the end of 2017.[1]

According to the Ipsos Ireland Social Networking report from September 2017, Instagram is used by 27 percent

---

1. Instagram, "Instagram's 2017 Year in Review."

Introduction

of the adult population in Ireland. Of those that have an account, daily usage is at 56 percent.[2]

General global demographic data shows that:

a. 80 percent of Instagram users are outside of the US.

b. Most Instagram users are between 18–29 years old (59 percent).

c. Six in ten online adults have Instagram accounts.

d. Female internet users are more likely to use Instagram than men (38 percent vs. 26 percent).

e. 32 percent of teenagers consider Instagram to be the most important social network.

f. 32 percent of Instagram users attended college.

g. 51 percent of Instagram users access the platform daily, and 35 percent say they look at the platform several times per day.

h. 95 million photos and videos are shared on Instagram per day.

i. Over 40 billion photos and videos have been shared on Instagram since its inception.[3]

---

2. Norton and Porter, "Social Networking—Aug 2017".
3. Lister, "33 Mind-Boggling Instagram Stats & Facts For 2018."

1

Defining Cyberspirituality

IN THIS LITERATURE REVIEW I have tried to look into past and present research about spirituality and the Internet, especially social media. There are a few different approaches: some scholars speak about "cyberspirituality," while others use the term "digital religion," and there is also a development of "cybertheology." I am looking into "secular spirituality" as well because, even though we don't have quantitative research to see the exact numbers, many people who post on social media about spirituality use such a discourse.

At the outset I need to clarify how I understand and use important terminology in this literature review. Firstly, having read more than 50 articles and books, my conclusion is that most authors (about 85 percent) have digital religion as their core focus; by digital religion, I mean research about how churches and religious communities use the Internet for communication and how their members talk about religion and religious values online. I will discuss this in more detail below.

Secondly, I have learned that many who use the term "cyberspirituality" are not really referring to spirituality but more to digital religiosity.

Thirdly, I wish to distinguish between "cyberspirituality" and "spirituality of cyberspace." By this I mean that the majority of authors write about the spirituality of the Internet as a place, and about the possibility of the Internet being a community—I would call that the spirituality of cyberspace. However, in my view the term "cyberspirituality" should be used for research about how people express, share, and live their personal spiritual values online.

Fourthly, cybertheology is an important relative term which has only emerged in 2014 and, while it is not a focus of research here, it will be important to mention it in the literature review.

Finally, when looking into the religious affiliation of people who use the Internet to post about spirituality, many belongs to the category of secular spirituality. I therefore outline my understanding of this phenomenon.

Up to this time an agreed definition of cyberspirituality has not been arrived at. It is not possible to choose some leading authors in the field. Instead, a lot of research that includes spiritual values or practices is done and classified as religiosity under the term "digital religion" and these two discourses often overlap. Cyberspirituality is therefore the area of main interest for my research.

1.1. CYBERSPIRITUALITY

There is no universal definition of cyberspirituality. The understanding of the term can be divided into two different discourses: spirituality of cyberspace (the spiritual dimension of the Internet) and cyberspirituality as a research of expressing and practicing spiritual values online. I see it as

Defining Cyberspirituality

a way in which people construct their digital identity and their spiritual identity as a part of it, and how they live that dynamic through their online activities and practices.

Cybergrace: the Search for God in the Digital World by Jennifer Cobb was one of the first books about the spiritual dimension of the Internet. Cobb stated that "as we reach into the future in search of the age-old spiritual values of the truth, beauty, goodness and love, cyberspace can be a powerful ally. Through the medium of computation, our spiritual experience can be extended in profound ways."[1] Cobb was writing about the spiritual dimension of the technology, which was later used to form this part of the discourse about cyberspirituality.

The Way, a journal for contemporary Christian spirituality, dedicated a whole issue (July 2000) to cyberspirituality. The authors were writing about the Ignatian prayer for Internet users, sacred space and time in the computer age, Internet and displacement, God in cyberspace, and spiritual direction in cyberspace. The discourse is one of spirituality of cyberspace, with questions about the tensions between virtual and real presence, the formation of communities online, the sacredness of cyberspace, and the ethical issues, and is mainly skeptical about possibilities of practicing spirituality online.

Ronan Tobin wrote an article in 2004 called "A Hitchhiker's Guide to Cyberspirituality." Analyzing the forms of spirituality that were emerging among users of the Jesuit website Sacred Space, he found out that Christian cyberspirituality is orthodox (users unite around the person of Christ), fundamentally dialogical (giving information through dialogue), pragmatically ecumenical (people pray together online and keep their offline traditions), anonymous (safe space for personal disclosure), life-integrated

1. Cobb, *Cybergrace*, 8.

(space for bringing the sacred into everyday activity), efficient (guidance and help always available); self-directed (takes effort to participate), communitarian (makes a real community) and missionary (a place not only for authentic spiritual experience but also for social action). Tobin argues that cyberspirituality does connect to real life and "cultivates encounter through connection" where technology is only providing a context.[2]

That is a move towards the discourse of cyberspirituality. In 2005, Heidi Campbell identified four common discourse strategies used in connection with religion and Internet technology: "a spiritual medium facilitating religious experience, a sacramental space suitable for religious use, a tool promoting religion or religious practice and a technology for affirming religious life." Campbell explains that, in the spiritual medium discourse, the Internet can be seen as a spiritual network, a place where users can come in their search for individual or communal spirituality: "Here the Internet is used to search out one's personal spiritual destiny that can be interpreted through a narrative of shared experience. It highlights the desire for freedom and spiritual experience that can be shared with others."[3]

In his 2007 book *Studying Christian Spirituality*, David Perrin argues that a "lot of soul exists in cyberspace, for cyberspace influences the deeper dimensions of being human."[4] Communicating with others without the limitations and realities of every-day life can bring a transcendental quality to virtual relationships, in a space where people can explore new aspects of the self. Perrin advises caution, noting it is difficult to determine the authenticity of others, and even of the virtual self, which creates an illusion of a

   2. Tobin, "Hitchhiker's Guide to Cyberspirituality," 591–97.
   3. Campbell, "Spiritualizing the Internet," 9–15.
   4. Perrin, *Studying Christian Spirituality*, 311.

Defining Cyberspirituality

meaningful relationship. In cyberspace, says Perrin, people can "experience themselves in disembodied form" but still have the real experience of embodiment—"gratification with instant communication, a sense of intimacy with the other or profound feelings of trust and being cared for."[5] Cyberspirituality is, for Perrin, the study of these shifts in self-perception, "the way the spiritual self is constructed, enlivened, and lived out"[6] and it is not just spreading religious information or evangelization.

However, there is still not enough research done in this direction. The way people use technology to express their spirituality significantly changed with smartphones. Practicing religion for many young people has shifted from being primarily in the public (such as churches and institutions) to the more private spaces of their everyday lives. In particular, the social platforms on digital devices are central to young adult identity. As "digital natives" (persons who are born and raised with the presence and use of Internet technology), young people perceive their devices and apps as a tool they may use for spiritual purposes as well.

The study of religious affiliation and practice among young Europeans aged 16–29, conducted by St. Mary's University in London and the Institut Catholique de Paris, has shown that just 2 percent of young Catholics in Belgium, 3 percent in Hungary and Austria, 5 percent in Lithuania, and 6 percent in Germany say they attend mass weekly. On the other side of the scale are their peers in Poland (47 percent), Portugal (27 percent), and the Czech Republic and Ireland (both at 24 percent). Some 54 percent of Irish people in this age bracket identify as Catholic, 5 percent as belonging to other Christian denominations, 2 percent as

---

5. Perrin, *Studying Christian Spirituality*, 312.
6. Perrin, *Studying Christian Spirituality*, 313.

being part of a non-Christian religion, and 39 percent say they have no religion.[7]

One of the consequences of this is a crisis of religious authority—users can be drawn to the pluralism of spirituality expressions and a possibility to share and discuss personal spiritual values rather than follow official religious figures or institutions. Helland says that the Internet has become the "unofficial religious environment"[8] and a study done among Christian and Muslim students of George Mason University in Virginia in 2016 discovered that religious apps have indeed replaced the roles of traditional religious leaders in the participants' lives. Students state that they would rather look to apps for guidance than talk to someone at a religious institution. Participants also stated that use of religious apps made spirituality a much more private experience for them than it was in the past. Spiritual life for them became less about the religious community they belong to or the actual relationships with others who share their faith, but more about how faith could be integrated into daily life.[9]

Religious people, even those who live a secluded monastic life, also use social media to communicate about their spirituality. Isabel Jonveaux analyzed 50 personal Facebook profiles of Austrian and German monks and nuns who live in contemplative monasteries and found that the number of friends they had was higher than the average friend count. Facebook profiles allow nuns and monks to present themselves in the world, and they post pictures of themselves in their habits and with the inclusion of their religious titles.

---

7. McGarry, "Young Irish People Among the Most Religious in Europe," lines 3–43.

8. Helland, "Popular Religion and the World Wide Web," 25.

9. Huges Rinker et al., "Religious Apps for Smartphones and Tablets," 1–14.

Defining Cyberspirituality

This gives monastic communities and monks the opportunity to create new visibility in a secularized society: "When monks post pictures of themselves playing football or sitting in a cinema wearing 3D glasses on their personalized Facebook walls, it gives a novel, plausible image of monastic life, which is no longer so much different to the one that people live in the world."[10] Many are also posting pictures of their spiritual activities and say they often receive private messages from young people with questions about life and faith.

Heidi Campbell argues that "in an era marked by social media we see that religious self-expression and representation has become an accepted part of religious identity and practice. As new media have become infused into our daily patterns, technology helps extend our abilities to integrate spirituality into our everyday lives in new ways."[11] For example, if you search for a meditation app in the Google play store in April 2018, you can choose between 252 applications to install on your smartphone. The ability to have such an app with you all the time and use it to meditate on the go, for example during morning commute, can change the way you practice your spirituality.

With social media, the Internet is not a separate space anymore; and the border between online and offline life and identity has become very fluid. If people express and live their everyday social life online, then to a similar extent, spiritual life is happening online as well. When lived and expressed online, spiritual narratives and practices are generally very flexible. Due to the challenges in data collection and copyright issues, there is very limited research done to date. Also, much of the research about spirituality and/or religion online is mostly qualitative. Methodologies for

10. Jonveaux, "Facebook as a Monastic Place," 99–109.
11. Campbell, *Digital Religion,* 10.

managing big data sets on social media platforms and new methods for data analytics are now necessary to go further: "There needs to be much more research on religious use of Facebook, Twitter, YouTube, Instagram, and religious apps to comprehend how these innovations have developed and impacted religious practices and understanding."[12]

1.2. DIGITAL RELIGION

In order to understand developments in cyberspirituality, it is necessary to locate the research within the wider field of digital religion. Religious discussions and content started to appear on the Internet about 30 years ago. That was the time of the so-called Web 1.0, the first stage of the Internet, which was entirely made up of more or less static websites that were not providing interactive content. Yet, users could visit online forums and engage in different discussions, so early studies focused on documenting religious practices, the creation of "virtual communities" and web-based houses of worship such as cyber-churches. The majority of the research has focused on different websites, especially the ones created by religious institutions or religious communities. Many researchers were looking into the world of gaming, and the main questions were about "the notion of religious community online, including what group interactions through an online forum or platform can truly be considered a religious community."[13]

In 2000 Christopher Helland came up with the distinction between two categories: Religion-Online and Online-Religion. Religion-Online was understood as importing

12. Campbell and Vitullo, *Assessing Changes in Digital Religion Studies*, 85.

13. Campbell and Vitullo, *Assessing Changes in Digital Religion Studies*, 74.

Defining Cyberspirituality

traditional forms of religion online. Online-Religion was uniquely secularly spiritual, claimed Helland, because it can create new forms of networked spiritual interactions and promote discussions of ritual and "awe"-filled moments within a secular, online community.[14] Because of the Internet's ability to cross social and cultural borders, Helland argued that the Internet has created a non-threatening environment which is ideal for users to engage in spiritual searching. Online-Religion could be, in that sense, better named as cyberspirituality, because it is not necessarily connected with traditional religious environments or communities.

According to Heidi Campbell, the first stage of the study of religion and the Internet, during the Web 1.0 stage, may be described as cyber-religion. In 2012 a new term emerged, and researchers began to talk about digital religion, "religion that is constituted in new ways through digital media and cultures."[15]

During the time of Web 1.0, research was focused on how users construct their virtual interactions, and how the online activity influences religious institutions. From 2004, the Internet is referred as Web 2.0. The way that websites were designed and focused changed, allowing users more interaction, collaboration, and sharing of information. The websites and applications which provide opportunities to create and share content are generally referred to as social media. More religious groups and institutions started to build their online presence and research had to move more into content analysis. Content was not anymore only textual, and there was a rise of religious content in different online games, such as *Second Life* or *World of Warcraft*. Highland and Yu declared that digital media, especially

14. Helland, *Online-Religion/Religion-Online*, 205–23.
15. Campbell, *Digital Religion*, 3.

video games, can create experiences that bring inner peace and help individuals to communicate about it with the use of mythology.[16]

Campbell and Vitullo notion that the research about religion and Internet can be divided into four stages:[17]

a. Stage one—descriptive stage

   The initial, descriptive stage focused on documenting how different groups were described, or described themselves, as religious communities online. Studies have focused on how the Internet affects specific communities, what strategies they use to gather believers online and saw the virtual spiritual life as separated from the offline activities. Researchers were looking into online prayer forums, chat groups, and other text-based websites.

b. Stage two—categorization stage

   In stage two, scholars focused on categorization, identifying the common characteristics of how community was performed and how the members related online. Most studies highlighted the positive potential and discovered that online communities were transforming the traditional meaning of community. There was a surge in the creation of cyber-churches, such as I-church, founded by the Church of England in 2004 as an experimental online community in the Benedictine tradition. Church of Fools was a four-month experiment launched in 2004, sponsored by the Methodist Church as the first 3D church. Users were able

---

16. Yu and Highland, *Spiritual Experience with Video Game Technology*, 268.

17. Campbell and Vitullo, *Assessing Changes in Digital Religion Studies*, 74.

Defining Cyberspirituality

to enter and move around, talk to others, pray, and attend services from various traditions.

c. Stage three—theorizing online and offline community practices

Beside online forms of religious community, offline religious communities started to use digital technologies for ministry work. This meant paying closer attention to offline religious communities' negotiation with new media and theorizing over online and offline community practices. Some examples include creation of religious versions of popular technologies such as GodTube.com and Millatfacebook.com, representing Christian and Muslim versions of YouTube and Facebook.

d. Stage four—current stage

Over time, researchers moved more towards detailed content analysis. Twitter was launched in 2006 and Facebook was launched in 2004, and both changed the way people expressed their religious identity and spiritual paths online. Current research tends to focus on the intersection of online and offline religious communities' practices and discourses. Most of the research now focuses on social media such as Youtube, Twitter, Facebook, and mobile apps.

The current phenomenon of social media popularity shows how much has changed in the building of one's identity; it now includes digital identity, as well as in the way we build our social relationships. Media studies scholar Vincent Miller observes that US and European ideals of community are derived "from a caricature of village life" that assumed limited geographic mobility, "rootedness in place and history" and the high levels of interdependency and social obligation.[18] Many people also identify themselves as members of a national community, which is formed around "symbolic resources (symbols, flags, anthems, sports teams, heroes) and nationally-based media (newspapers, television, literature, history)."[19] In contrast to these village-based and national conceptions, digital culture is the space that promotes "networked individualism" and its character is based on choice rather than geographic location, open-ended opportunities for belonging, engagement, and acceptance. In the online form, communities are hosted mainly on social networks. They are new community spaces, where one can get to know and meet people. We can choose who we want to know and follow, considering common interests and ways of thinking.

Research done among more than 1800 adolescents in Catalonia in 2016 looked into the significance of social media as a platform for expressing religion in adolescence. The most-used social networks are Instagram (78 percent), Facebook (71 percent), Google (68 percent), YouTube (60 percent), and Snapchat (60 percent)—so mostly image-based networks. Data has shown that 16 percent of the interviewed youth use or practice digital religion. Of them, 57 percent use it for communicating with other people, 43 percent for doing academic projects, 37 percent to learn more about their religion, and 30 percent to be aware of activities organized by their communities. 28 percent search for images and videos about their religion, while 20 percent want to learn about other religions. One important finding was: young people admit they use or practice digital religion only if they are sure that the people who they connect with share the same beliefs. Data shows that 64 percent of adolescents who use or practice digital religion do not tell

18. Miller, *Understanding Digital Culture*, 186.
19. Miller, *Understanding Digital Culture*, 187.

their friends that they do it; the 8 percent who admit they do, only tell about their use or practice of digital religion to those who share the same faith. 14 percent of young people reported that they use their digital devices to pray.[20]

1.3. CYBERTHEOLOGY

Some authors and researchers use the term cybertheology as a way of mapping religious topics in their engagement on the Internet. In many ways, cybertheology is also the study of spirituality as expressed on the Internet and of the everyday representation and imagination of the sacred, but from the point of view of religious institutions or authority figures.

Antonio Spadaro, Jesuit priest and journalist, in his 2014 book *Cybertheology*, tried to assess the impact of social media and digital technologies on theology. He offered a new definition, saying "it is necessary to consider Cybertheology as being the intelligence of the faith in the era of the Internet, that is, reflection on the thinkability of the faith in the light of the Web's logic."[21] Spadaro compares cybertheological reflection to the listening to and reading of the Bible, a reflexive knowledge that starts from the experience of faith: "Cybertheology is not, therefore, a sociological reflection on religiosity on the Internet, but is the fruit of faith that frees from itself a cognitive impulse at a time when the Web's logic marks the way of thinking, knowing, communicating, and living."[22]

Spadaro sees social networks not only as an ensemble of individuals but as an ensemble of relationships between

20. Díez Bosch et al., "Typing My Religion," 121–43.
21. Spadaro, *Cybertheology*, 16.
22. Spadaro, *Cybertheology*, 17.

individuals, which means that the main concept of the Internet is no longer just presence, but connection. Public space has been moved to the territory of the smartphone and this will influence the idea of the local church as well, changing the way that ecclesial communities are built.

Pope Emeritus Benedict XVI dedicated several messages—written for World Communication Days—to digital technology and social media. He sees them as a help to foster dialogue which can unite individuals and promote harmony: "If the networks are called to realize this great potential, the people involved in them must make an effort to be authentic since, in these spaces, it is not only ideas and information that are shared, but ultimately our very selves."[23] For Benedict it is clear that "the digital environment is not a parallel or purely virtual world but is part of the daily experience of many people, especially the young."[24] He was calling for creativity and imagination, and the use of art, music, and attentiveness.

The digital identity and activity of Pope Francis has also been a subject of study for cybertheology. Damian Guzek analyzed the papal Twitter account (@pontifex) for six months between 2013 and 2014. He focused on 135 tweets published during that time to see how the papal authority is presented and shaped online. His second question was what the strategy of the papal account is. The results showed the picture of papal authority typical for the offline world, and the data indicated that the strategy was mainly an appeal for social topics and reflective discourse. Interestingly, although the author uses the term "religion" when analyzing the content in his work and concludes that the pope is addressing Catholic believers, some of the results show that Francis is also often posting about spiritual values.

23. Benedict XVI, "Social Networks."
24. Benedict XVI, "Social Networks."

Defining Cyberspirituality

According to categories, the content of the papal tweets was about Jesus Christ (15.91 percent), forgiveness (6.06 percent), God's love (5.30 percent), Lady Mary (4.55 percent), Christian activity (4.55 percent), Christmas (3.79 percent), prayer (3.79 percent), throw-away culture (3.03 percent), holiness (3.03 percent), people in need (3.03 percent), trust to the Lord (3.03 percent), others (3.03 percent), spreading the joy of Christianity (3.03 percent), peace (2.27 percent). Other categories, with less percentage, include topics such as communication, neighbors, the elderly, faith, education, talents, family, community, smiling, unity, authenticity, gospel. and mercy.[25]

Theo Zirdejveld analyzed the current pope's Instagram account (@franciscus) and personal branding. At the time of the study (April 2017), Francis had 4.2 million followers. Today that number is 5.2 million. Zirdejveld points out an interesting fact that the name of the Instagram account is not connected to the office of the pope (like @pontifex on Twitter) but to the name of the person (@franciscus), which makes the Instagram more personalized. When religious organizations use the marketing techniques of branding, their leaders often become personifications of their religious communities and have to compete in a spiritual marketplace. Zirdejvejd analyzed two photos published during the visit to Egypt and concluded that the pope derives authority on Instagram from the fact that people are interested in his actions and statements, which is in numbers much more than most other religious figures receive.[26]

In the last few years, there are many books being published on cybertheology, especially from a pastoral perspective of a certain Christian religious community or church (I believe they cannot classify under cyberspirituality, as

25. Guzek, "Discovering the Digital Authority," 63–80.
26. Zirdejveld, "Pope Francis in Cairo," 125–40.

they are all coming from a point of a particular theology). Some of the most popular are: *Beyond Me, My Selfie & I: Finding Real Happiness in a Self-absorbed World* by Catholic journalist Theresa Tomeo; *Viral: How Social Networking Is Poised to Ignite Revival* by Protestant theologian and pastor Leonard Sweet; *Tweet If You Love Jesus: Practicing Church in the Digital Reformation* by theologian and spirituality scholar Elizabeth Drescher; and *#Struggles: Following Jesus in a Selfie-Centered World* by Craig Groeschel, who is a founder of Livechurch.tv.

Some authors, like Sweet and Drescher, hold a very positive attitude towards social media, recognizing the cultural change in communication and identity, finding social media as a new opportunity for religious institutions, church leadership, and individuals to reconnect and live their faith. Both authors recognize some difficulties that older generations have in adapting to this new culture and they offer insights and advice on how to use social networks effectively.

Other authors, like Tomeo and Groeschel, warn about the selfie culture and claim that use of social media leads to an inauthentic, superficial life with people losing control of their life and spirituality. They both argue that self-worth and finding true love should not depend on the number of likes got on social media and they discuss the challenges of being authentic online. At the same time, they draw a clear line between online and offline identity and relationships, saying that faith can only truly be lived offline.

1.4. SECULAR SPIRITUALITY

While I have focused on faith and religion in the above discussions, it is important to note that cyberspirituality may be secular in character. According to the philosopher

Defining Cyberspirituality

Jay Newman, "technology's very success is contributing to the realization of ideals such as freedom, knowledge, happiness, and peace."[27] These are spiritual values, and a secular spirituality that embraces these values is often embraced by people who identify as "spiritual but not religious."

In today's society, there are people who describe themselves as spiritual, although they do not want to be members of traditional religions or follow their doctrines. "Secular spirituality is neither validated or invalidated by religious varieties of spirituality,"[28] notes Peter H. Van Ness in the book *Spirituality and the Secular Quest*, a volume in the World Spirituality Series. The criteria to be spiritual does not have to be a belief in Jesus or membership of a religious community, it is rather "an attribute of the way one experiences the world and lives one's life."[29] We can see examples of that in the rising popularity of different mindfulness programs, especially the ones developed for a workplace, as well as in different ecological or social justice movements whose roots are not religious but whose motives are spiritual.

The origins of secular spirituality in the West can be traced to ancient Greek and Roman philosophers, influences from Asian civilizations, and the discoveries from the Enlightenment period. The postmodern phenomenon of New Age spirituality introduced the notions of self-spirituality, ecological spirituality, feminist spirituality, gay spirituality . . . This shows that not everything spiritual must be religious because "there are ways of understanding the world as a cosmic whole and the self as an enduring agent that are not directly indebted to religion."[30] Van Ness

27. Newman, *Religion and Technology*, 110–11.
28. Van Ness, *Spirituality and the Secular Quest*, 1.
29. Van Ness, *Spirituality and the Secular Quest*, 2.
30. Van Ness, *Spirituality and the Secular Quest*, 7.

also points out that secular spirituality can help traditional religions in recognizing their common concerns and can serve as a sort of mirror, helping with revitalization of religious spiritual traditions.

Secular spirituality can also have an impact on our humanistic value system. In an individualized society, people are inclined to search for better versions of themselves (their true self), looking for similar-minded individuals who share the same values outside of traditional settings and sometimes even deeply provoking the traditional value settings. Some examples include holistic or alternative medicine programs (i.e. chiropractic, homeopathy) or "Twelve Step Programs" for Alcoholics Anonymous.

Thomas Moore, former monk and author of the book *A Religion of One's Own: A Guide to Creating a Personal Spirituality in a Secular World,* claims that many who left religious institutions, as well as people who were raised without religion, hunger for more but do not want to follow organized religion's path to spirituality. He offers the solution of creating a personal spiritual style, either inside or outside of formal religion. His advice includes regular meditation, ethical living and working, responsibility, dream practice and mysticism, intimacy with nature, adding monasticism into daily life, aiming for bliss, developing personal philosophy and theology, and learning from religions and spiritual traditions, even without joining, in order to combine the secular and sacred.[31] Moore's description provides a comprehensive outline of a secular spirituality and it may be the case that much of cyberspirituality will belong to this category.

---

31. Moore, *A Religion of One's Own*, lines 7–25.

2

Spirituality and Selfie Culture

POSTMODERN CULTURE HAS CHANGED the way people think about their spirituality, and social networks have changed the way they communicate about it.

While the use of the term "spirituality" becomes more and more detached from traditional beliefs, it does refer to the human search for the deepest values and sense of meaning: "Spirituality embodies some kind of vision of the human spirit and of what will enable people to achieve their fullest, even transcendent potential."[1]

Sherry Turkle, a psychologist who is doing the research in MIT about online identity since the mid-1970s, argues that the Internet is a clear postmodern phenomenon, characterized as "decentred," "fluid," "nonlinear," and "opaque." This is contrary to the modernist terms of "linear," "logical," and "hierarchical." By enabling the reconstruction of self, the Internet has become a social laboratory for people to experience multiple identities, not as permanent

1. Sheldrake, *Spirituality*, 8.

structures in the mind but as conversational and relational ways of being. Identity is no longer viewed as unitary and autonomous but can be decentered, multiple, and fluid as long as it's integrated: "Without any principle of coherence, the self spins off in all directions. Multiplicity is not viable if it means shifting among the personalities that cannot communicate."[2] For Turkle, the flexible self is characterized by inner communication between the various aspects of selves and nourishes the respect for diversity.

Thomas L. Friedman, three times Pulitzer winner and a columnist for *The New York Times,* has a very interesting point of view about God and cyberspace in his book, *The Lexus and the Olive Tree.* Friedman says that, because the most popular content online has nothing to do with spirituality (but with pornography, gambling, music, etc.), if we look at God as someone who endlessly intervenes through divine acts, then there is no God in cyberspace. Friedman, coming from his personal Jewish tradition, says that his view on God is post-biblical: "We are responsible for making God's presence manifest by what we do. And the reason that this issue is most acute in cyberspace is because no one else is in charge there. There is no place in today's world where you encounter the freedom to choose that God gave men more than in cyberspace . . . God is not in cyberspace, but He wants to be there—but only we can bring Him there by how we act there."[3]

It is very difficult to say what the ultimate interior motives of people who post about spirituality on social media are, and whether they belong to the category of traditional believers or not. Therefore, spirituality frameworks for this research are drawing from the idea of authentic subjectivity—people posting about their own personal spiritual

2. Turkle, *Life on the Screen,* 258.

3. Friedman, *Lexus and the Olive Tree,* 469.

quests by—sort of—journaling on the Internet and finding the spiritual in secular moments, things, and relationships.

2.1. SELFIE CULTURE

Taking self-portraits is nothing new—people have been doing that for centuries, changing techniques from painting to photography. With the rise of smartphone use and the development of numerous social media platforms, taking a selfie has become regular practice for millions of people around the world.

According to the Oxford Dictionaries, a selfie refers to "a self-portrait photography of oneself (or oneself with other people), taken with a camera or a camera phone held at arm's length or pointed at a mirror, which is usually shared through social media."[4] Selfie was pronounced the "Word of the Year 2013" for the increased frequency of its use. The term can be traced back to 2002 when it was used in an Australian online forum, but gained popularity throughout the English-speaking world in 2013 as it evolved from a social media buzzword to mainstream use.

339,516,078 Instagram posts by April 3, 2018 had a #selfie hashtag.

The number of deaths while trying to produce a great selfie is rising from year to year, so that there is a page on Wikipedia counting and describing selfie-related accidents. In 2015, Russian police started a campaign called "Safe selfies," warning against standing on railroad tracks, climbing onto roofs, or posing with a gun or a tiger.

What are the reasons for producing selfies? There are many possible personal motives, for example producing an intimate souvenir, making a journal entry out of a moment,

4. Oxford English Dictionary. "Selfie." https://en.oxforddictionaries.com/definition/selfie.

projecting a desirable image and memory for future generations, crying out for help, or just for fun. The *International Journal of Mental Health and Addiction* published a study in 2017 which explored the concept and collected data on the existence of "selfitis" (obsessive taking and publishing of selfies). Authors also identified six factors behind selfie producing:

1. environmental enhancement ("taking selfies gives a good feeling to better enjoy the environment and provides better memories about the experience")

2. social competition ("taking selfies helps to increase social status," e.g., "I post selfies to get more likes and comments")

3. attention-seeking (e.g., "I feel more popular when I post my selfies," "I gain enormous attention")

4. mood modification (e.g., "I am able to reduce my stress level," "Taking selfies instantly modifies my mood")

5. self-confidence (e.g., "I feel confident," "I become more positive about myself")

6. subjective conformity (e.g., "When I don't take selfies, I feel detached from my peer group")[5]

However, not all the attention on selfies has been negative. For instance, some psychologists argue that selfies are a healthy form of self-exploration, allowing individuals to be more authentic.[6] It is very interesting that, even though many reasons for taking selfies are based on the need to fit in and get approval from the peer group, the main motivation

---

5. Balakrishnan and Griffiths, "Exploratory Study of "Selfitis,"" 722–36.

6. Rutledge, "#Selfies," lines 56–64.

is actually capturing the moment and expressing one's feelings. Excessive use of social media and posting selfies can, however, have negative implications for one's self-image, identity, mental health, and social relationships. It can lead to a so-called "head down" habit, when people bury their heads down in their smartphone screens, communicating with technology even if they are sitting next to each other.

Another problem we encounter today is that the Internet can allow the fantasy principle to cover reality—it is very easy to be someone you are not, and that alternative persona is usually much more perfect than the real you, warn Jean Twenge and W. Keith Campbell in *The Narcissism Epidemic: Living in the Age of Entitlement*. Through images and brief self-description, people place attention on the shallower aspects of their persona, and people who are desperate for attention have a huge potential audience on the Internet: "An increasing number of Americans not only admire fame from afar but fervently wish to enter the circle of celebrity themselves. In 2006, 51 percent of 18-to 25-year-olds said that 'becoming famous' was an important goal of their generation—nearly five times as many as named 'becoming more spiritual' as an important goal. A 2006 poll asked children in Britain to name 'the very best thing in the world.' The most popular answer was 'being a celebrity.' 'Good looks' and 'being rich' rounded out the top three, making for a perfectly narcissistic triumvirate. 'God' came in last."[7] As one of the solutions, authors propose the practice of gratitude, as opposed to entitlement: "you think about what you already have, instead of what you deserve to have but don't."

GenX and millennials are the generations who first embraced technology development and represent the majority of users on social media. Considering the average

7. Twenge and Campbell, *Narcissism Epidemic,* 93–94.

lifespan is 27,375 days, an average millennial is expected to take 25,700 selfies during their lifetime. That's almost one selfie per day. 55 percent of social media selfies come from millennials, but Gen X follows with 24 percent and baby boomers with 9 percent.[8]

2.2. SPIRITUAL BUT NOT RELIGIOUS

In *The New Metaphysicals: Spirituality and the American Religious Imagination,* Courtney Bender looks into practices of people who identify as spiritual but not religious. They can sometimes be spiritual, sometimes religious, and sometimes secular, as we can see in the example of yoga. According to Bender, the religious experience is reproduced in secular discourse about the self and private belief. Spiritual practices are not any more primarily located within religion or other fields such as art or science, but they can evolve in multiple locations, being universal. Bender talks about spirituality as a process of looking forward, happening in places that are not traditionally religious. Spirituality is today created and lived at the crossroads of different secular realms such as art, health, and vacation, entangled in daily life as well as existing in the traditional religious houses of worship.

Linda Mercadante, in *Belief Without Borders: Inside the Minds of the Spiritual but Not Religious,* analysed the results of her qualitative study of about one hundred people who identify as 'spiritual but not religious'. She confirmed that "non-affiliation or disaffiliation from religion is especially common among younger people, and it is unlikely that this is merely a youthful rebellion or a temporary phase."[9]

8. Galuppo, "Millennials Are Expected to Take A Massive Number of Selfies," lines 7–10.

9. Mercadante, *Belief Without Borders,* 244.

Spirituality and Selfie Culture

Her research shows that people who identify as spiritual but not religious are not nihilistic or anarchistic, not against belief, but are very open to theological questions. They view religious/political/financial institutions as tainted by wrong values and self-interest, and articulate the trouble in finding ones that match with their spiritual beliefs. Spiritual but not religious tend to describe religion as "institutional," "dogmatic," "exterior," and "unessential," while they view spirituality as "personal," "private," "open," "individualistic," and "core." They want to keep their spiritual options open and look less for committing and affiliating, but more for exploring and choosing. They express longing for authentic, meaningful relationships, willingness to care about community and civic life, commitment to valuing inclusivity, and a search for genuine experience.

The "spiritual but not religious" category has now in the Western world been confirmed as a sort of spiritual revolution—more people are spiritually searching now than previously. Spiritual seeking is on the rise across generations; many are searching for meaningful spiritual practices and for a vital spiritual community.[10]

According to the 2017 report by Pew Research Center, about a quarter of US adults (27 percent) now say they think of themselves as spiritual but not religious. This number is rising among men and women, different ethnic groups, people of different ages and education levels, and people from different political spectrums. In addition to those who say they are spiritual but not religious, 48 percent say they are both religious and spiritual, while 6 percent say they are religious but not spiritual.[11]

10. Mercadante, "Understanding the Spiritual but Not Religious," slides 28–32.

11. Lipka and Gecewicz, "More Americans Now Say They're Spiritual but Not Religious," lines 7–31.

Spirituality in the Selfie Culture of Instagram

In most of the Western world, the spiritual but not religious adherents belong to either the so-called Generation X (generations born between 1965 and 1980) or millennials (born between 1981 and 1996). In *GenXReligion,* Richard Flory and Donald Miller found out that members of this generation tend to favor experiential faith and communion with God that is achieved through activities such as dancing and yoga. They also pointed out that Gen Xers like to merge lifestyle and religious expression in a kind of mixture of the sacred and the profane, especially in music and the arts.

Neil Howe and William Strauss coined the term "millennial" when they first sought to describe the children of the baby boomers and older Gen Xers. Compared to Generation X, millennials have the highest percentage of religiously non-affiliated people of any previous generation in recent American history. According to the Pew Research Center, 35 percent of adult millennials are religiously unaffiliated. Far more millennials say they have no religious affiliation compared with those who identify as evangelical Protestants (21 percent), Catholics (16 percent) or mainline Protestants (11 percent). In comparison, 70 percent of Generation X identified with some Christian faith and only 23 percent identified as religiously non-affiliated.[12]

Findings from the Pew Research Center, however, show that religiously unaffiliated Americans or "Nones"—defined as those who identify as atheist, agnostic or "nothing in particular"—still have a lot of spirituality. For example, a quarter (26 percent) of religiously unaffiliated Americans say they meditate regularly. Even among self-described atheists, about one-in-five (19 percent) meditate weekly or more often, an indication that not all people who meditate

---

12. Lipka, "Millennials Increasingly are Driving Growth of Nones," lines 10–18.

Spirituality and Selfie Culture

do so for religious reasons.[13] Believing in God, reading the Bible, or attending religious services for the "Nones" are not essential to being a moral person, but it is by being honest and grateful that a person is truly moral. Additionally, 23 percent mention the golden rule (treating others as one would wish to be treated), kindness, empathy, and love as traits of a moral person. Other attributes include being tolerant and helpful to others and being true to self.[14]

The 2016 Irish census showed that while Ireland remains a predominantly Catholic country, the percentage of the population who identified as Catholic has fallen, while the number of people with no religion grew. Those with no religious affiliation now account for almost 10 percent of the population, making them the second biggest group in the country.[15] Other research, done as an exit poll report for the 2016 general election, provided the choice between atheist, agnostic and the category "I'm not religious, although I do consider myself a spiritual person." While only 1 percent identified as agnostic and 4 percent as atheist, 9 percent of those surveyed said they were spiritual but not religious.[16] This can lead to the implication that this is a rising category of people in Ireland, as well as in the US.

In the research project, "Religious vocations in Ireland: challenges and opportunities," Noelia Molina has

13. Masci and Hackett, "Meditation Is Common Across Many Religious Groups in the U.S.," lines 32–35.

14. Pew Research Center, *Religion in Everyday Life*. http://www.pewforum.org/2016/04/12/essentials-of-christian-identity-vary-by-level-of-religiosity-many-nones-say-honesty-vital-to-being-a-moral-person/.

15. Central Statistics Office. "Census 2016 Summary Results." https://static.rasset.ie/documents/news/census-2016-summary-results-part-1-full.pdf.

16. Central Statistics Office. "2016 Exit Poll Results." https://static.rasset.ie/documents/news/rte-exit-poll-report.pdf.

built a religious/spiritual picture of Ireland today. Based on the World Values Survey, the largest cross-cultural study of changes in cultural beliefs, values, and worldviews, Molina states that in almost all industrial and post-industrial societies values have shifted from traditional (religion and family are important) to secular (religion, traditional family values, and authority are less important). In terms of cultural values, Ireland does not fit into Catholic Europe; rather it belongs to the cultural values of the English-speaking world. This shift is especially notable among young generations who have "a market mentality that has emerged directly from the process of postmodernism. Postmodern thinking allows the discrediting, critique and discounting of everything. The younger generation, especially 18–29 years old are post secular, in the sense that there is an increase in 'believing without belonging.'"[17]

Molina's research points out that the young generation "is not particularly interested in institutions but is open and receptive to spiritual authenticity and genuine narratives of experience." It states that the main challenge in vocations is to respond to the call of the times to keep connecting and relating to younger people. The way to do it: social media. Participants in the study highlighted the importance of personal spiritual narrative shared on the Internet, especially mentioning blogs, Twitter, Facebook, and YouTube.

2.3. DYNAMISM OF AUTHENTICITY AND GLOBAL SPIRITUALITY

There are many people today who by witnessing their authenticity on social media represent great inspiration to others, such as Pope Francis for example, with more than

17. Molina, *Religious Vocations in Ireland*, 7.

5 million followers on Instagram. For Easter, the Church of England encouraged followers to share photos of baptisms, services, and church celebrations using the hashtag #EasterJoy on all forms of social media. On Facebook, the page "Ask a Catholic Nun" has almost 270,000 followers and the Dalai Lama has a Twitter account since 2008, now with 17.3 million followers. The Instagram account @Placesyoullpray shows Muslims praying in all the corners of the Earth, including in front of the Auschwitz memorial.

The spiritual framework for this research was inspired by Michael O'Sullivan's concept of authentic subjectivity. According to O'Sullivan, the foundation for understanding humans as spiritual beings is their inner dynamism which attracts a person towards beauty, truth, goodness, and love.[18] It is in the core and nature of every person and therefore we can presume that there is also a desire to communicate it.

O'Sullivan says that "the dynamism of authenticity functions through the following four basic operations of consciousness: experiencing, understanding, judging, and deciding, and that the corresponding norms of consciousness inherent in these respective operations are: be attentive, be questioning, be critical, and be responsible and loving."[19]

Understood as such a process, authenticity means living open to data, seeking information, desiring to find truth and love, living in an open dynamic way, and being ready to change if needed. It is an open-ended process, a process of change, living for wherever truth, beauty, goodness, and love might lead a person.

My question for this research was: how do people, and do they at all, express a desire for beauty, truth, goodness,

18. O'Sullivan, "Reflexive and Transformative Subjectivity," 173–82.
19. O'Sullivan, "Authenticity as a Spiritual Process."

and love through posting photos and using hashtags on Instagram? To be able to study spirituality, we must assess the quality of inner operations in experiencing, understanding, judging, and deciding. By using hashtags, Instagram users are self-defining the message and meaning of their images and opening a channel to communicate about it.

Taking a photo, capturing a moment in time, and sharing it on the Internet can be seen as a sort of spiritual journaling, mapping their inner dynamism of authentic subjectivity. With the Internet and social media, the world is becoming more integrated. Information technology makes it much easier for like-minded individuals and small groups to create spiritual communities. They can be positive and help with building bridges toward others, but they can also stay like small isolated islands, satisfied with their own beliefs and convinced in their righteousness. So, first of all, when talking about cyberspirituality, we have to be good listeners.

The focus in developing authentic subjectivity is in its quality. This dynamism can clash with our previous traditions or our relationships, our ties with institutions or authorities. The dynamism of authenticity brings in the critical view on the events in our life and challenges us to examine our relationships by the standards demanded by authenticity.

This challenge means having to look into our spiritual lives through this process of questioning, and not, for example, through the fulfillment of devotional practices demanded from us by our religious community or tradition. For example, one's personal spirituality does not have to be interlinked with whether you go to church every Sunday or not. It can also be a move from the image of a punishing God, who demands that we follow strict rules posed by his representatives on Earth (church leaders, holy fathers, etc.)

Spirituality and Selfie Culture

into the image of a loving God who can be found in nature or through the kindness of others. This does not have to mean that we must completely reject our religious traditions or that the only way to God is outside of any kind of community. One can live their authentic spirituality as a member of the church or religion, if they live it through the dynamism of authenticity.

Cyberspirituality can also be global spirituality. Jack Finnegan, in *The Audacity of Spirit: The Meaning and Shaping of Spirituality Today,* talks about the emerging of contemporary spiritualities. They are often abstract visions from traditional religions—Christian, Jewish, Buddhist, Hindu, Taoist, Confucian, and Islamic—merged with modern, ecological, economic, feminist, or pacifist practices: "Spirituality shows clear signs of becoming a global enterprise grounded in global thinking and appealing to a global community."[20] However, even if global spirituality can cross religious, political, and cultural divisions it is unlikely that we will see the emergence of a worldwide syncretic religion or spirituality, says Finnegan. Spirituality needs a context, whether local or global, and needs to affirm the reality and ethical demands of the world, "the shaping demands of social otherness and difference, of social and ecological engagement and solidarity, of self-sacrifice,"[21] even if these practices are not popular in the late-modern vision of self.

---

20. Finnegan, *Audacity of Spirit*, 44.
21. Finnegan, *Audacity of Spirit*, 78.

3

Spirituality on Instagram

It is challenging to study spirituality on the Internet, not only because of its many definitions but also because of a partial lack of organized communities, traditions, and practices, which would make it easier to observe and analyze. Mostly, when talking about spirituality on social media, we need to take the content which users themselves labeled as spiritual or connected to spirituality—in other words, something which is self-assessed and reported as such. The multiple uses and interpretations of the term make it difficult to identify what spirituality is or to classify the people who identify themselves through it, as well as to understand its effects.

Social media language is different from everyday language—it is short, to the point, and very often reduced to only one word, called a hashtag. Oxford Dictionaries define hashtag as "a word or phrase preceded by a hash sign (#),

Spirituality on Instagram

used on social media websites and applications, especially Twitter, to identify messages on a specific topic."[1]

On Instagram, hashtags are used to define and/or describe the photo posted. They also serve to categorize the images, thus making it easier to be searched for and discovered later. Instagram users can "follow" other accounts, usually personal friends, celebrities, institutions, etc. In order to find and connect with new people or to engage in communication, they have to use hashtags. Since November 2017, Instagram offers the possibility to follow hashtags as well, not only accounts.

Every user keeps the copyright of his or her posted images. Including images in this research would necessarily mean getting usage permissions for each and every one of them. Therefore, this research cannot analyze the visual content of images. Users label their photos by using hashtags (thus giving them a name or description, giving words to the image content or mapping a category for the photo) so this research has to limit itself to the analysis of hashtags.

The research method did not include gathering of any personal data from the Instagram users and none was stored, therefore there was no need for any consensual forms from the users. There were no ethical issues for the research, and it was given an ethics approval after the initial proposal.

The research was designed to combine both qualitative and quantitative analysis. Based on the spirituality framework, it was decided to analyze these ten hashtags:

- #spirituality
- #God

1. *Oxford English Dictionary.* "Hashtag." https://en.oxforddictionaries.com/definition/hashtag.

- #pray
- #meditation
- #blessed
- #grateful
- #truth
- #love
- #kindness
- #liveauthentic

Hashtag #spirituality was chosen to establish the data within the field of cyberspirituality. Hashtag #God was chosen to take a look into the connection of personal spiritual relationship and the divine. For the further look into the spiritual framework of authentic subjectivity, the chosen hashtag was #liveauthentic. The reason for choosing this specific hashtag is the fact that hashtag #authentic is mostly used when posting about fashion and goods, in a sense of describing and differentiating original products from fake or counterfeit goods. Additional hashtags #truth, #beauty, and #love have also been chosen in connection to authentic subjectivity. Other hashtags: #pray, #meditation, #blessed, #grateful, and #kindness have been chosen as spiritual practices used in all religions but also within the framework of secular spirituality.

For the quantitative analysis I decided to use the software from the website Hashtracking[2] based in the US. The free trial option allowed the following of hashtags for a period of three days, starting on April 3, 2018. The monitored days were not representing any spiritual or religious holidays worldwide (when the number of posts would be higher than usually). The approach used to analyze the data

2. See: https://www.hashtracking.com/.

was visual methodology. Formally it would be referred to as document analysis, which has also expanded to video and photos.

Gillian Rose, in *Visual Methodologies: An Introduction to the Interpretation of Visual Materials,* suggests that "the visual" is key in the "cultural construction of social life in contemporary Western societies."[3] We are bombarded daily with images whose content can range from news events, advertisements, fictional stories, reality television, and personal stories. The key point Rose makes is that the production of images is never innocent. Images are not "transparent windows" but rather interpret and represent the world. Therefore, the qualitative visual analysis used here is also a discourse analysis, using the spirituality framework of authentic subjectivity.

3. Rose, *Visual Methodologies*, 6.

Spirituality in the Selfie Culture of Instagram

#SPIRITUALITY

2,884 posts with #spirituality were captured. They gathered 4,006 comments. More than 11 million people have seen the photos, which have been displayed more than 14 million times and got 84,778 likes.

Spirituality on Instagram

The most popular buzzwords about #spirituality are wisdom, love, yoga, inspiration, life, universe, enlightenment, self-love, spirit, faith, energy, healing, and law of attraction.

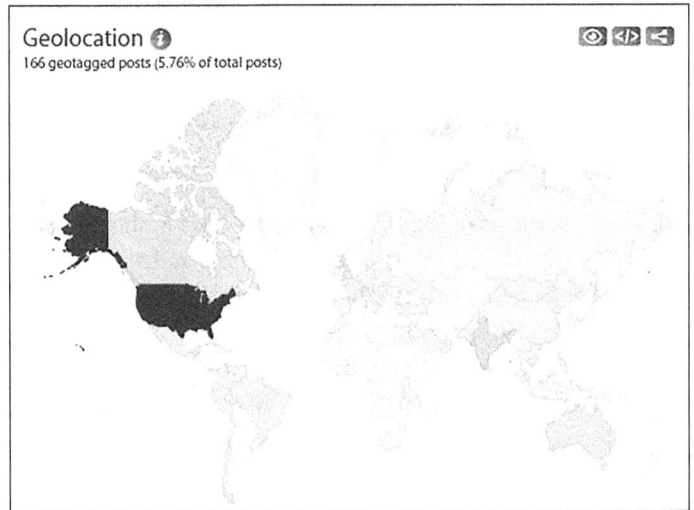

Spirituality in the Selfie Culture of Instagram

Only 5.76 percent of the posts were tagged. The 10 countries with the biggest number of posts were the US (85), the UK (12), India (12), Canada (9), Australia (5), France (5), Italy (5), Turkey (3), Poland (2), and Brazil (2). There were no posts from Ireland but there was 1 post from China.

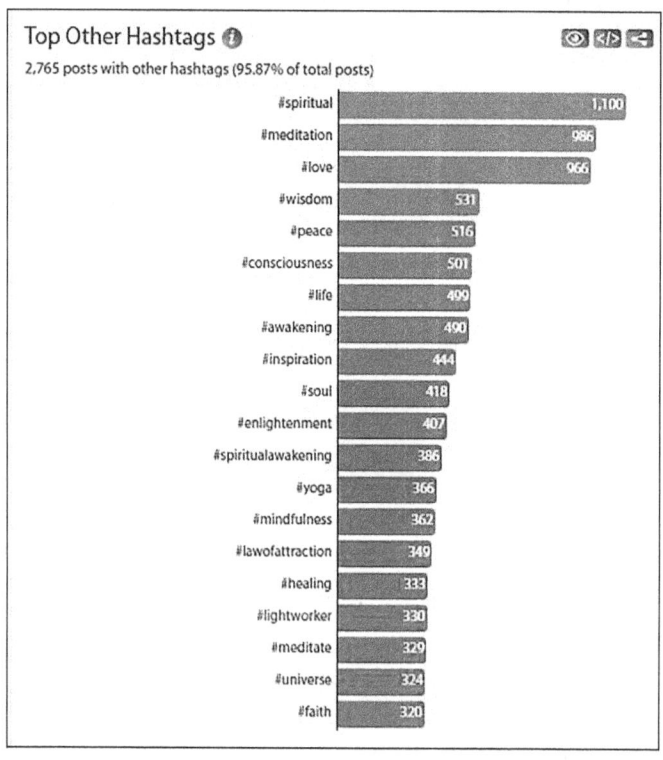

Almost all the posts (95.87 percent) had extra hashtags, the top 3 of them being #spiritual, #meditation, and #love.

The gathered data is showing that spirituality is a word people are posting about on a daily basis.

The emerging themes from buzzwords indicate that people are talking about personal and universal spirituality (love, wisdom, peace, consciousness, life, awakening,

Spirituality on Instagram

inspiration, enlightenment, universe, faith), not necessarily connected with any particular religious tradition. Emerging practices for spirituality are mostly meditation, yoga, and mindfulness—there is no mention of prayer for example. Another theme, present both in buzzwords and used as a hashtag is "law of attraction"—New Age philosophy especially popularized by Rhonda Byrne's book *The Secret*. On social media it is mostly connected with teachings from Ester and Jerry Hicks (Abraham Hicks). #Lightworker and #healing is used by people running or following different New Age spiritualities as well, for example angel spiritualities, etc. People are using #spirituality in English from all over the world, not only in English-speaking countries.

Spirituality in the Selfie Culture of Instagram

#GOD

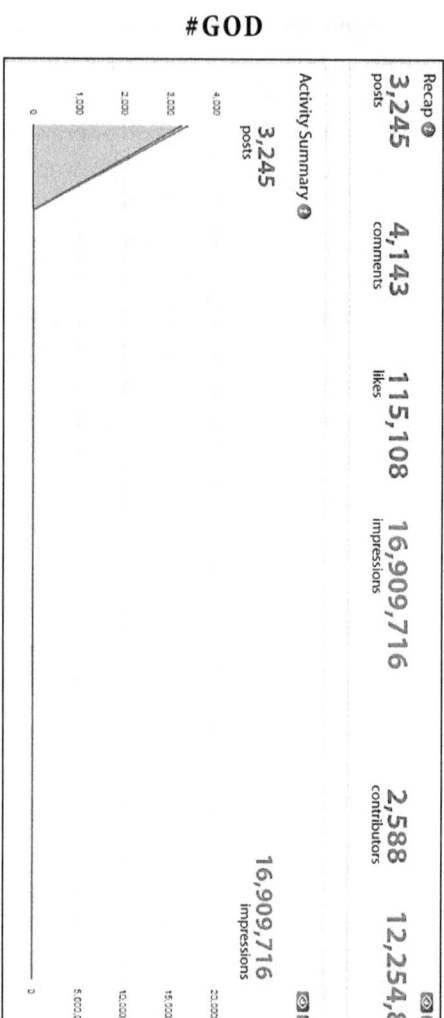

3,245 posts in 3 days had the hashtag #God. They gathered 4,143 comments and 115,108 likes. More than 12 million people have seen the photos, which have been displayed almost 17 million times.

Spirituality on Instagram

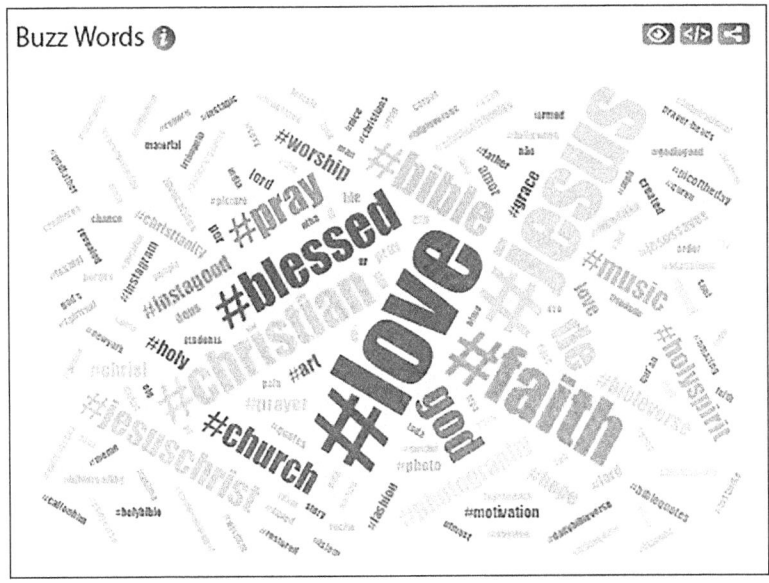

The most popular buzzwords about #God are love, Jesus, faith, Christian, Bible, blessed, church, worship, music, Holy Spirit, and photography.

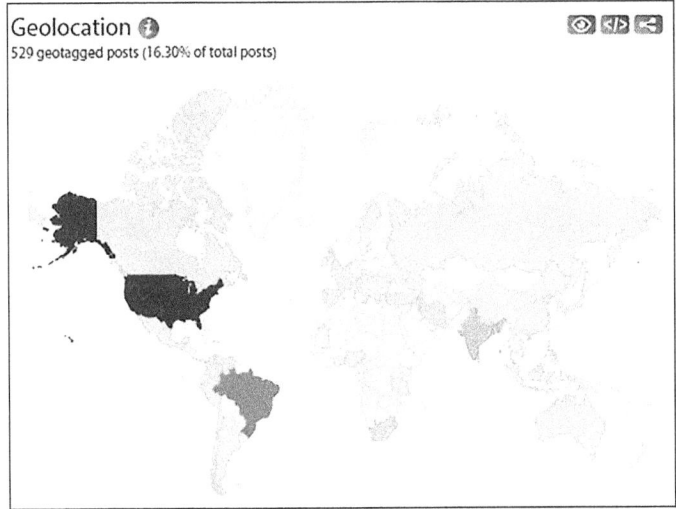

16 percent of the posts were geotagged. The 10 countries with the biggest number of posts were the US (171), Brazil (112), India (42), South Africa (22), Iran (15), Canada (11), UK (10), Venezuela (10), Turkey (7), and Germany (7). There were 2 posts from Ireland with #God.

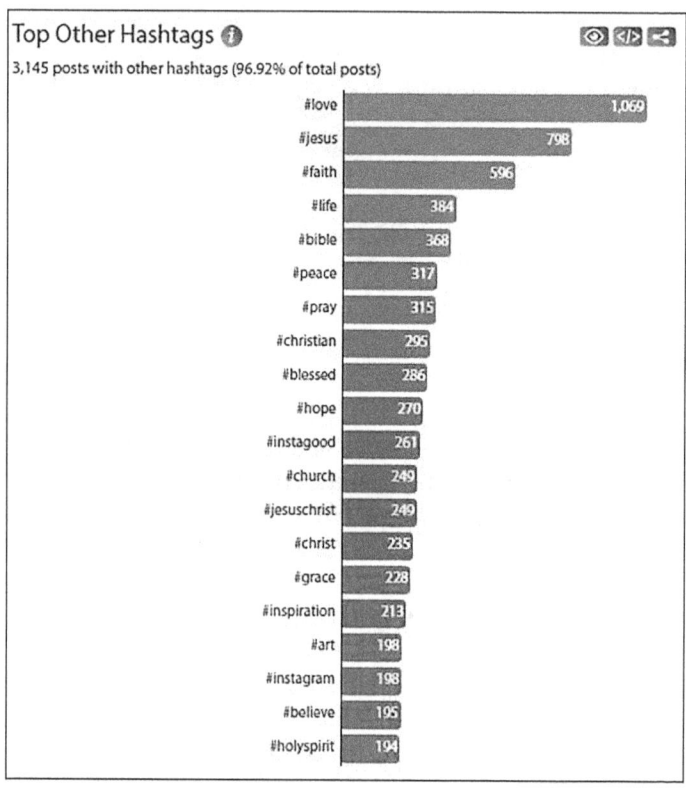

Almost all the posts (96.92 percent) had extra hashtags, the top 3 of them being #love, #jesus, and #faith.

The gathered data is showing that God is also a popular word on Instagram, with dedicated posts daily. The emerging theme from the buzzwords is showing that when people use the word God, they are talking about the Christian God and Christian spirituality (Jesus, Bible, church). This Christian spirituality is for them also the source of love, grace, salvation, motivation, and hope.

Emerging practices mentioned are prayer, worship, and music. Users are also expressing feeling good (#instagood), blessed, and inspired. Another emerging way of expressing thoughts and beliefs about God is #art and #photography. People are posting in English about God all over the world. The biggest number of posts, after the US, came from Brazil, India, South Africa, and Iran.

Spirituality in the Selfie Culture of Instagram

#PRAY

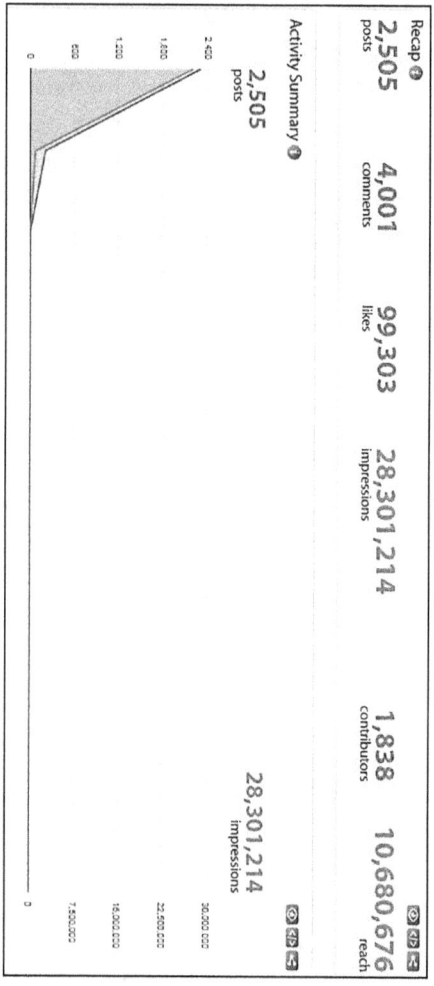

More than 10 million people have seen 2505 posts with #pray and they were displayed more than 28 million times. They got 4,001 comments and 99,303 likes.

Spirituality on Instagram

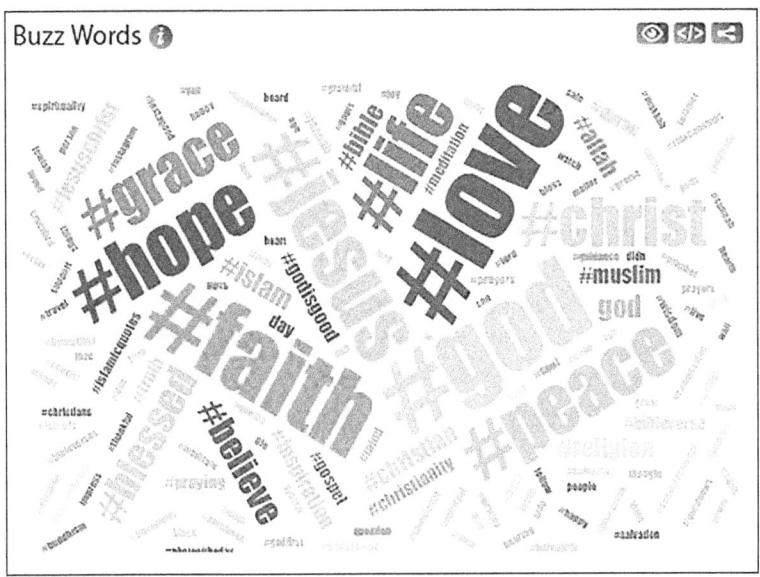

Buzzwords associated with #pray are either universal (faith, hope, grace, peace, believe, life) or distinctive by religious tradition (Jesus, Christ, Bible, Islam, Muslim, Allah, Quran).

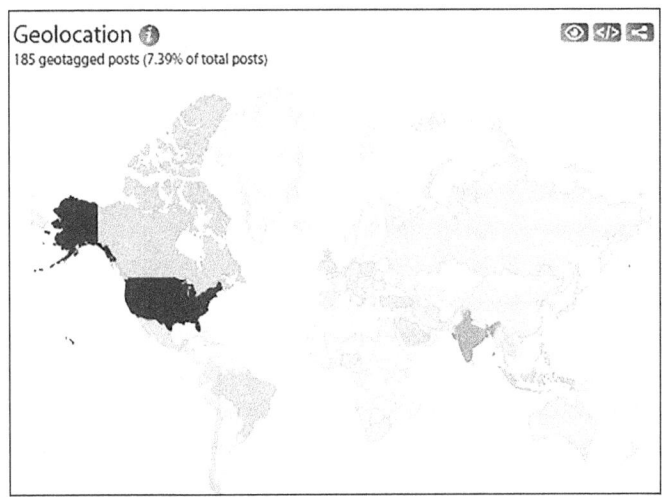

Spirituality in the Selfie Culture of Instagram

Only a very small number of posts showed the location (7.39 percent). The 10 countries with most of the posts were the US (68), India (29), Canada (11), Indonesia (10), Brazil (9), Saudi Arabia (8), the UK (5), Colombia (5), Italy (5), and Turkey (5). There was 1 post from Ireland during the observed period.

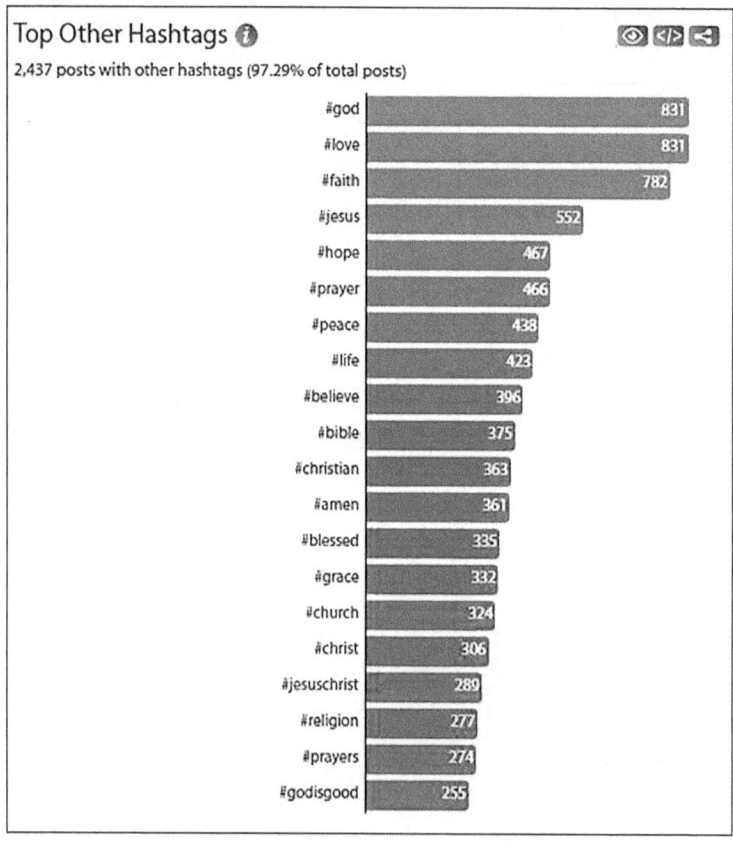

97.29 percent of posts had extra hashtags and the top 3 were #God, #love, and #faith.

The gathered data is showing that people are often using Instagram to post photos about praying. There are two

Spirituality on Instagram

things to be noted from the buzzwords and other hashtags. Firstly, when posting about prayer, users are noting their religion and naming a God they are praying to. In this case, we have an image of the Christian God (Jesus, Christian, Christ) but there is also a clear presence of prayer in the tradition of Islam (Allah, Islam, Muslim). Secondly, prayer is being connected with the acclamation that #Godisgood and the spiritual source for love, hope, peace, life, and grace. There are no emerging practices which would show what kind of prayer users are posting about, but both religions' sacred books are being mentioned (Bible, Gospel, Quran) which shows that people are using sacred texts to pray or quoting them in connection to the particular situation. Muslims from around the world are using the English word #pray—there are posts coming from Indonesia, Saudi Arabia, and Turkey.

#MEDITATION

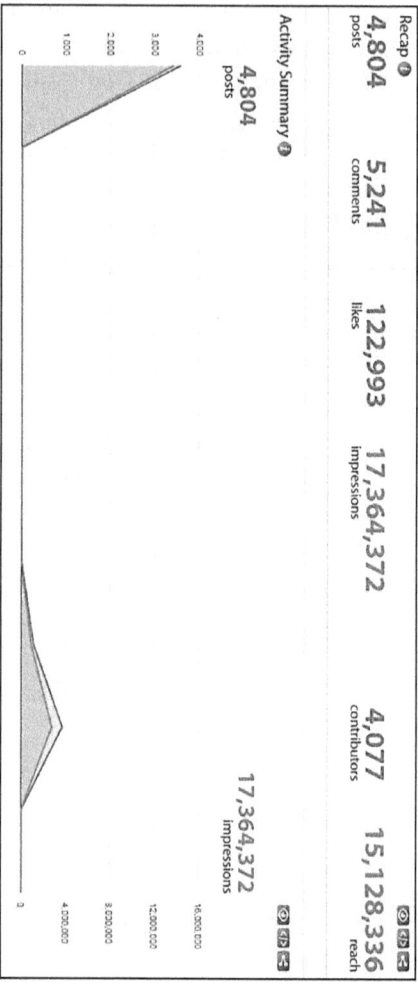

For 3 days, 4,804 posts with #meditation were noted. They gathered 5,241 comments and got 122,993 likes. More than 15 million people have seen the photos, which have been displayed more than 17 million times.

Spirituality on Instagram

Popular topics linked with #meditation are yoga, love, mindfulness and spiritual(ity).

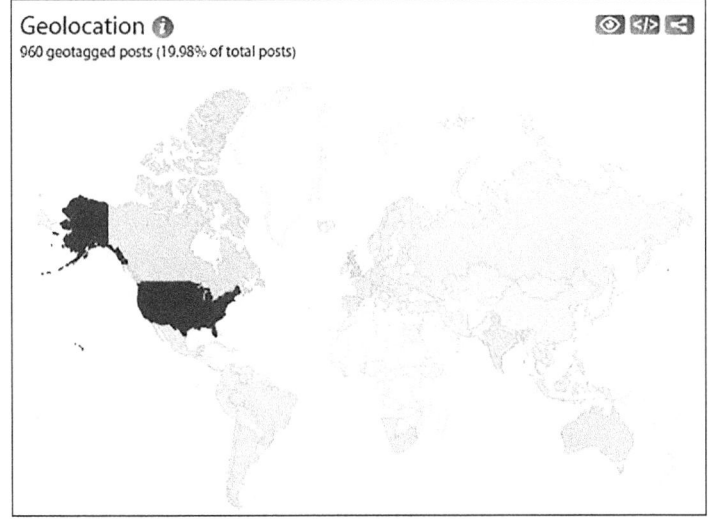

Spirituality in the Selfie Culture of Instagram

Almost 20 percent of posts showed the location. The top 10 countries by the number of posts were the US (432), the UK (64), Canada (49), India (36), Germany (27), Spain (25), France (22), Thailand (20), Brazil (17), and South Africa (13). There have also been 10 posts from Iran and 2 from Ireland.

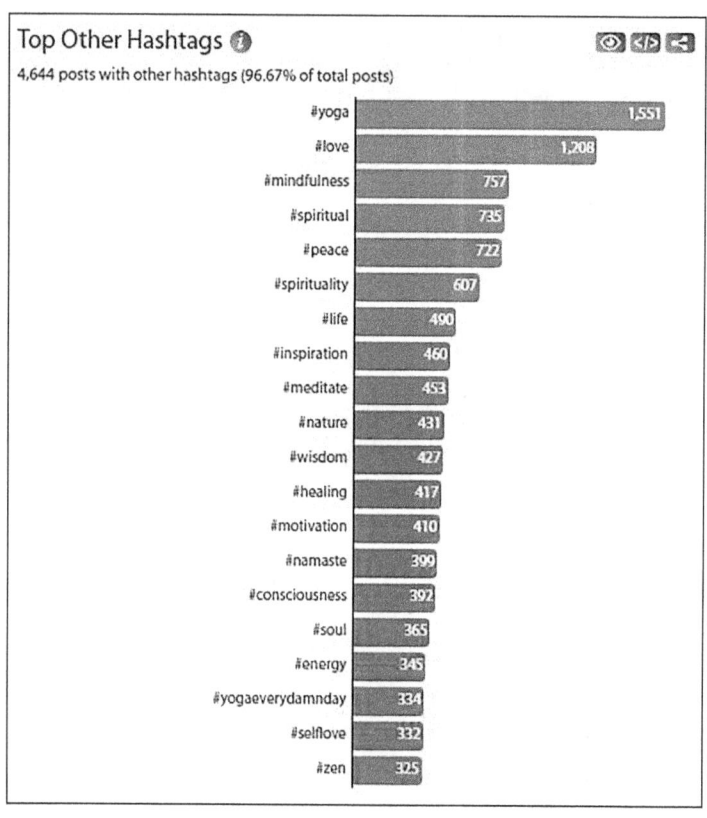

96.67 percent of posts had extra hashtags, the top 3 being #yoga, #love, and #mindfulness.

Meditation is the most frequent hashtag monitored—almost 5,000 posts in three days. It is frequently joined by #spiritual (735 posts) and #spirituality (607 posts), which shows that people associate meditation practice as an important part of spirituality, often in order to build #selflove (332 posts). Several emerging themes can be seen from the buzzwords: nature spirituality (travel, nature, explore), spirituality of the East (Buddha, enlightenment), and personal spirituality (awakening, inspiration, motivation, wisdom). #Zen and #namaste are also used as additional hashtags. Emerging practices connected with meditation are yoga and mindfulness. Use of the word #travel among the buzzwords shows that people are often posting about #meditation while traveling to other countries—there are posts from India and Thailand for example—but the majority of posts are coming from Western countries.

Spirituality in the Selfie Culture of Instagram

#BLESSED

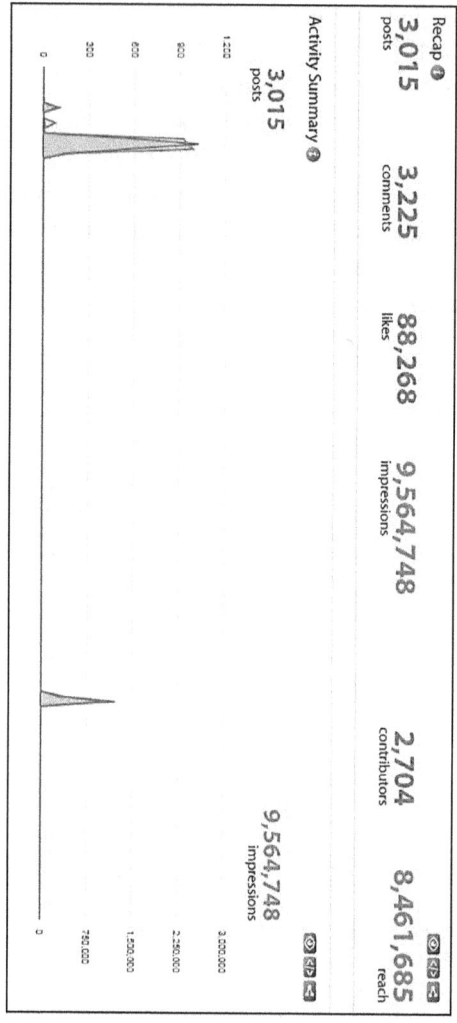

3,015 posts in three days had a hashtag #blessed. They gathered 3,225 comments and 88,268 likes. More than 8 million people have seen the photos, which have been displayed 9.5 million times.

Spirituality on Instagram

Popular buzzwords around the #blessed are feeling #love and #motivation, as well as being #happy. People also use #blessed in connection to strength and when they post about their personal image.

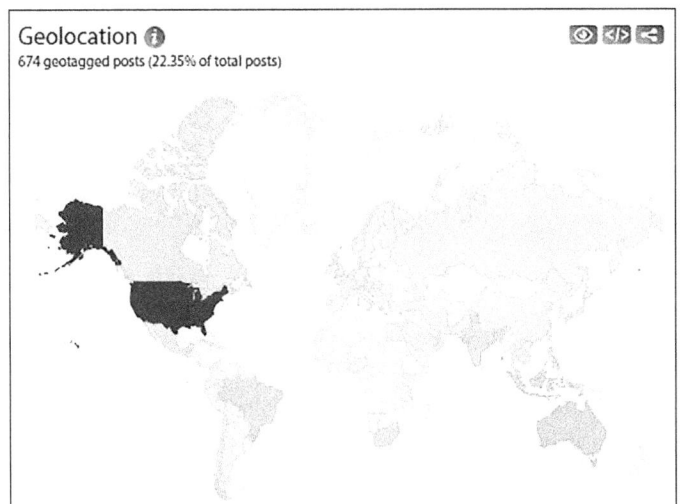

Spirituality in the Selfie Culture of Instagram

22.35 percent of the posts revealed the location from which they were posted. The 10 countries with most of the posts were the US (245), Australia (45), Brazil (37), Indonesia (35), Malaysia (31), India (28), Philippines (23), South Africa (22), the UK (20), and Canada (17). There were also 3 posts from Ireland.

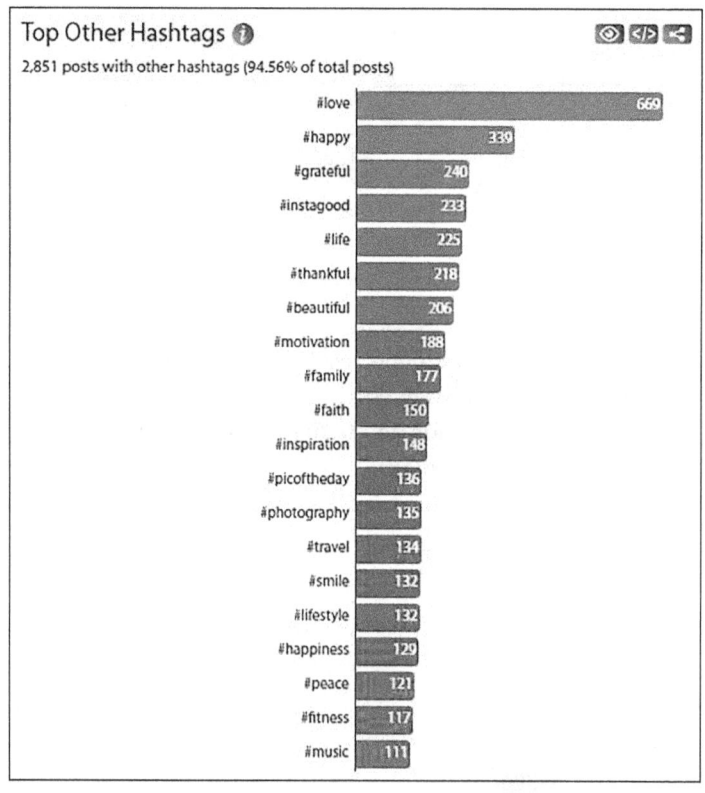

94.56 percent posts had extra hashtags and the top 3 were #love, #happy, and #grateful.

Emerging themes are showing that people feel blessed when they think about their looks and the beautiful things they have—material objects (#pretty, #fitnessmotivation,

Spirituality on Instagram

#fashion, #photography, #picoftheday, #lifestyle, #flowers). The feeling of being blessed was also linked with female strength (#strongwomen, #staystrong, #confident, #motivation). Blessings are also expressed when people feel love and happiness, especially for or from their family (#love, #baby, #life, #birthday). The notion of faith is present in 150 posts and the emerging spirituality practice we can see as being #grateful and #thankful. Music, travel, and photography are used as creative ways to express feeling blessed. A new location group emerged from this hashtag—people from South Asia and Indonesia are often expressing this feeling.

Spirituality in the Selfie Culture of Instagram

#GRATEFUL

More than 10 million of people have seen 2,679 posts with #grateful and they were displayed 10 million times. They got 3,750 comments and 97,436 likes.

Spirituality on Instagram

Buzzwords connected with #grateful are feeling #love and #blessed around #people, #friends and #family, or at #work.

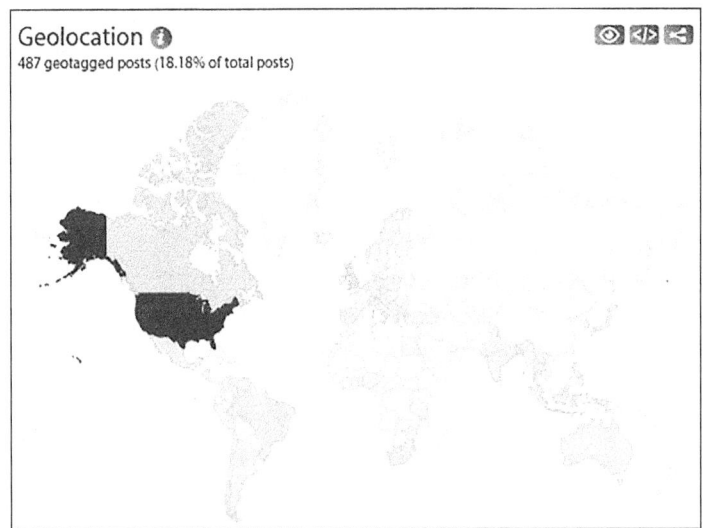

Only 487 posts showed their location. The top 10 countries by the number of posts were the US (224), the UK (30), Canada (29), Italy (17), Germany (15), Indonesia (15), Japan (13), South Africa (12), Brazil (12), and India (9). There were also 2 posts from Ireland.

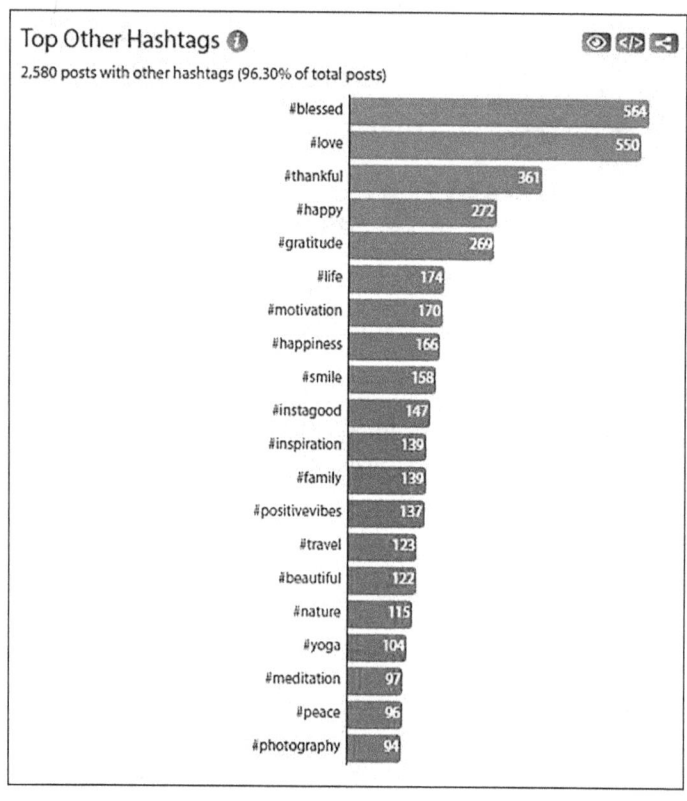

96.30 percent of total posts used additional words, most frequently #blessed, #love, and #thankful.

People who are #grateful are also feeling #love, #blessed, and #happy. From the buzzwords and other hashtags there are three different settings for gratefulness—work, nature, and family and friends. Spiritual practices

Spirituality on Instagram

mentioned with the feeling of being grateful are yoga and meditation, and there are also mentions of God and peace, so we can talk about personal and nature spirituality.

Even though hashtags #blessed and #grateful are often linked together (564 times) the difference is that these people are not expressing gratefulness for material things but for other people, especially family and friends. Being grateful also brought a new country on the list—Japan—while other posts came from South Asia, Western Europe, and the Americas.

Spirituality in the Selfie Culture of Instagram

#TRUTH

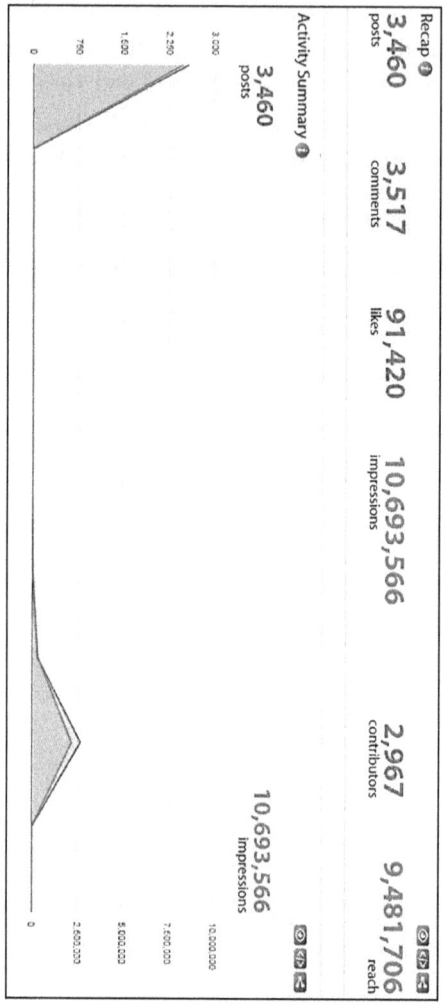

3,460 posts in three days had the hashtag #truth. They gathered 3,517 comments and 91,420 likes. More than 9 million people have seen the photos, which have been displayed 10.6 million times.

Spirituality on Instagram

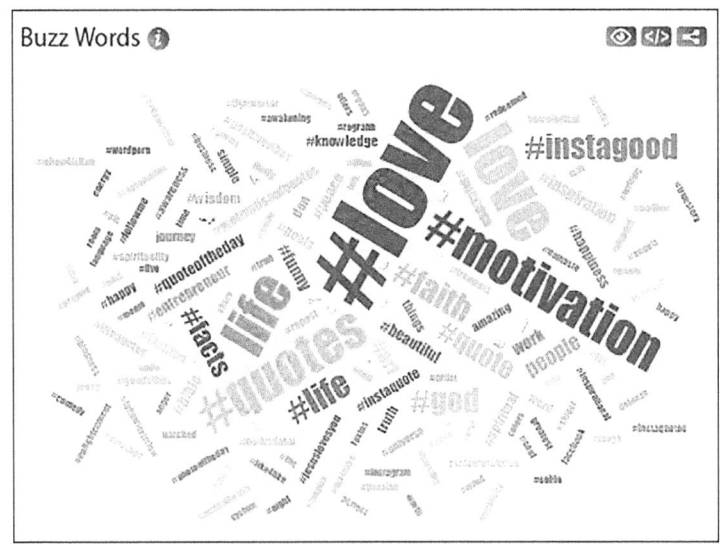

Buzzwords around #truth are #love, #motivation, #life, #faith, #good, and #quotes.

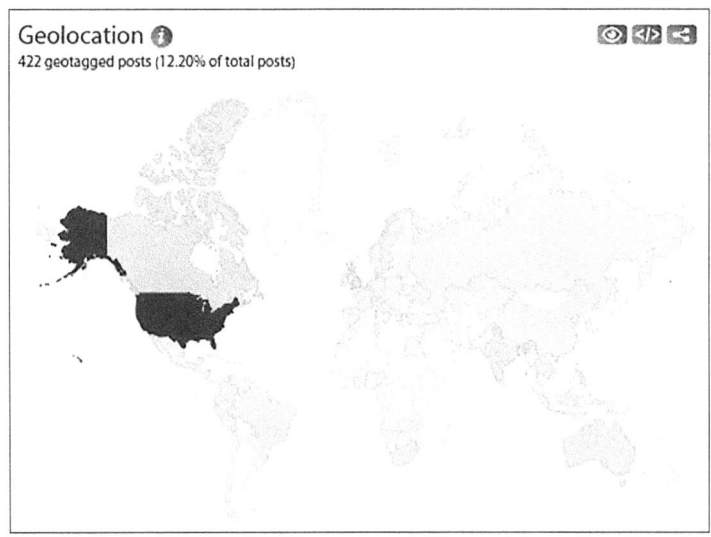

Spirituality in the Selfie Culture of Instagram

12.20 percent of posts were geotagged. The 10 countries with most of the posts were USA (272), Canada (25), UK (23), India (17), Indonesia (10), Italy (9), Netherlands (7), Norway (5), South Africa (5) and China (2). No posts from Ireland were shown.

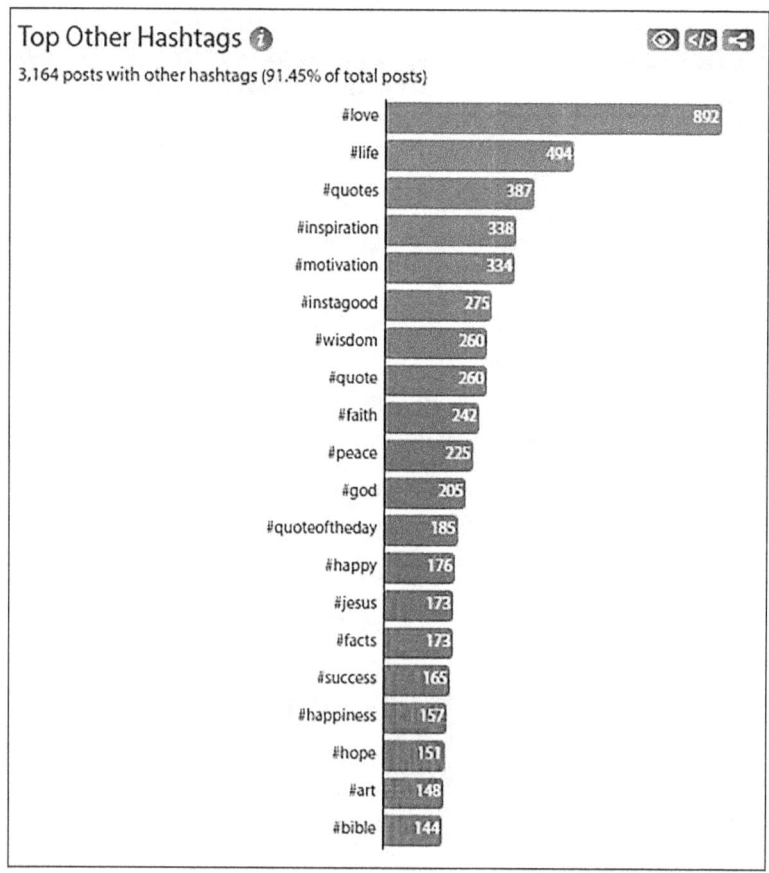

91,45 percent of posts used other hashtags, and the top 3 were #love, #life, and #quotes.

As a word on Instagram, #truth is not about politics or history (as we would find on other social media networks, especially Twitter), but emerging themes are life, love, faith, and knowledge. Faith is mentioned 242 times, God 205, Jesus 173, and Bible 144, so we can say that people are using the hashtag #truth when they are sharing about their Christian spirituality. They are also talking about the #journey and sharing a thought: #Jesuslovesyou. #Truth is also often used under different quotes in order to find inspiration, motivation, wisdom, hope, and happiness. Sometimes it's mentioned with some facts, and sometimes it is used when sharing artwork.

Spirituality in the Selfie Culture of Instagram

#LOVE

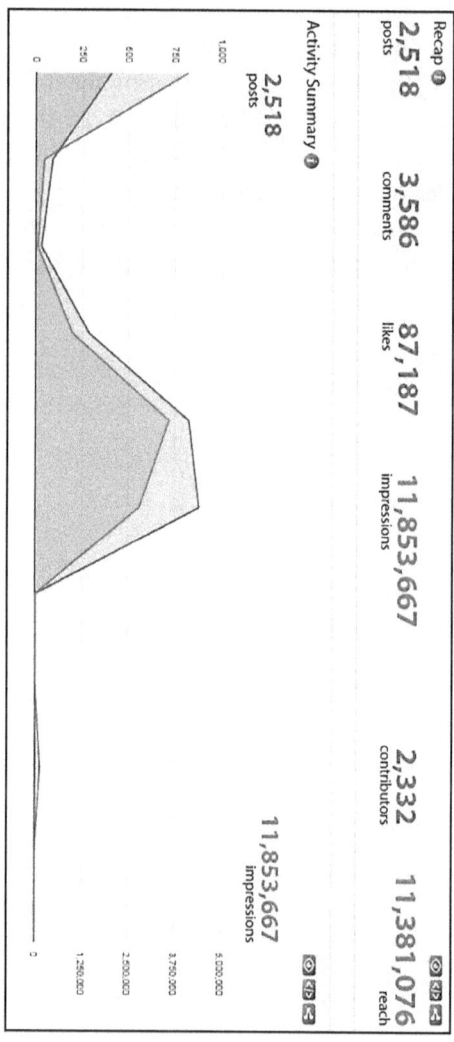

More than 11 million people have seen 2518 posts with #love and they were displayed 11 million times. They got 3,586 comments and 87,187 likes.

Spirituality on Instagram

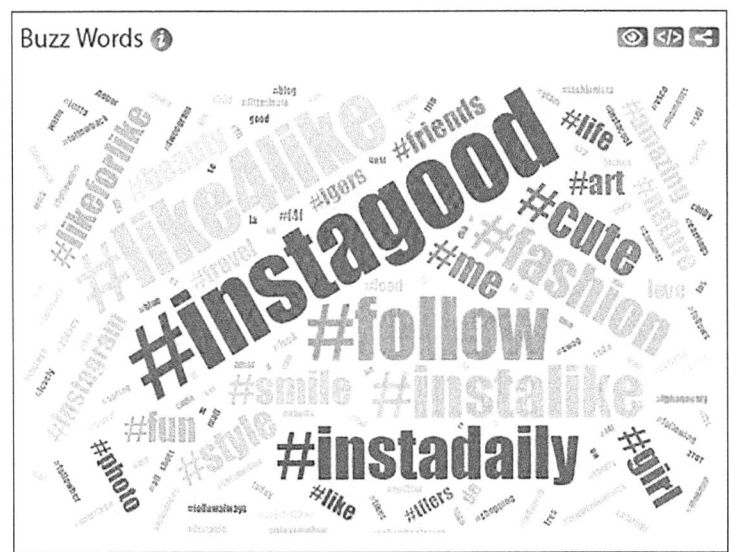

Buzzwords around #love are typical hashtags with high reach on Instagram, which people use to get more followers and likes: #instagood, #follow, #instadaily, #instalike, #like-4like, #cute.

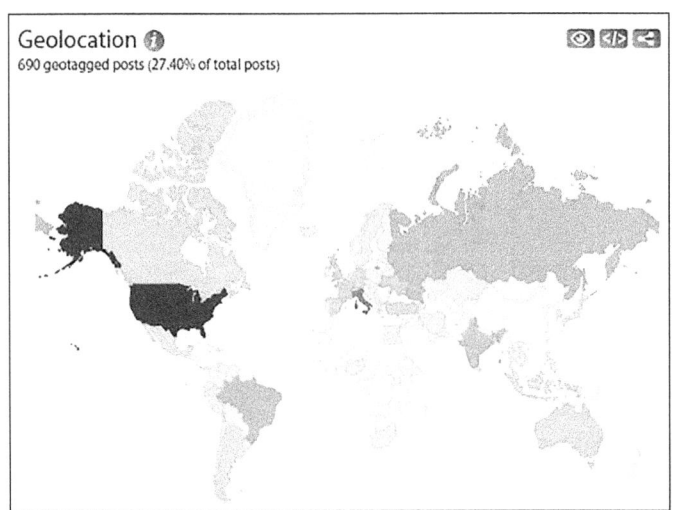

27.40 percent of posts showed the location data. The 10 countries with most posts were the US (112), Italy (77), Brazil (42), Russia (40), Ukraine (38), India (35), France (29), the UK (27), Turkey (22) and Germany (22). No posts were from Ireland.

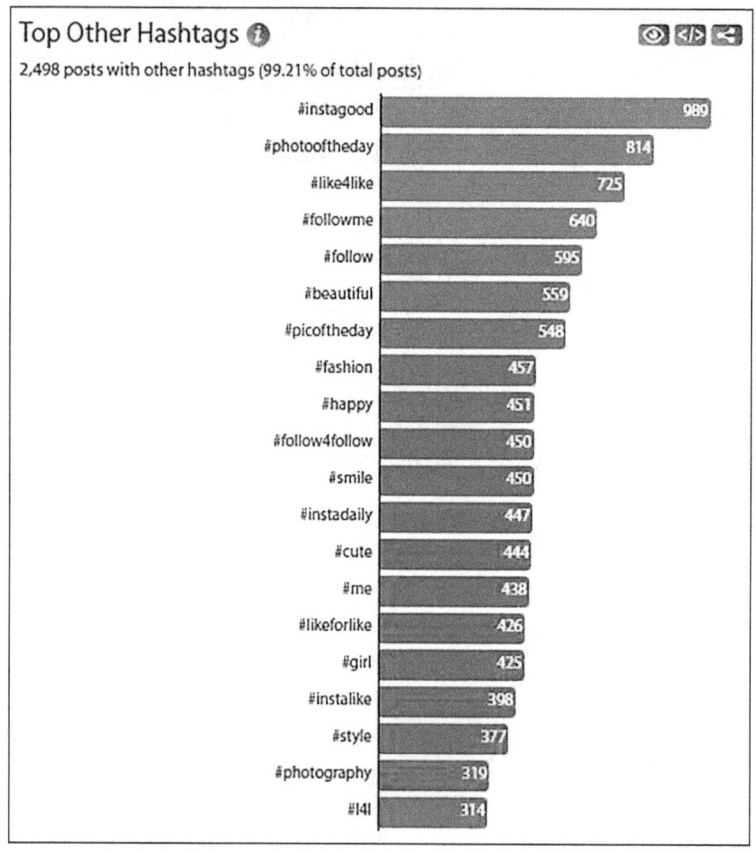

99.21 percent of posts had additional hashtags and most frequently used were #instagood, #photooftheday, and #like4like.

Spirituality on Instagram

Although #love is always used in connection with other hashtags which include the theme of spirituality, when used for itself #love is not a hashtag talking about spirituality in particular. It's mostly used by women (#girl, #beautiful, #cute, #fashion, #happy, #smile) in a photo form of a selfie (#me) to get likes and followers—all the buzzwords and other hashtags are used for that purpose.

Spirituality in the Selfie Culture of Instagram

#KINDNESS

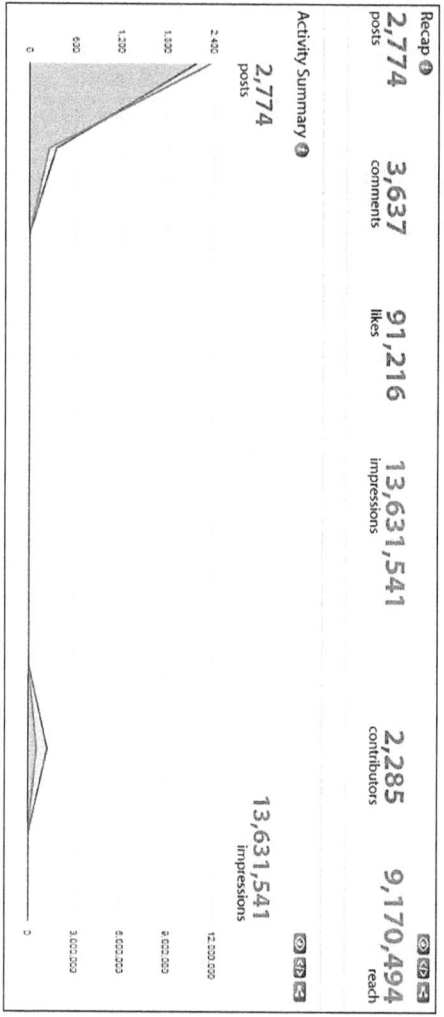

2,774 posts in three days had a hashtag #kindness. They gathered 3,637 comments and 91,216 likes. More than 9 million people have seen the photos, which have been displayed 13.6 million times.

Spirituality on Instagram

Buzzwords around #kindness are #love, #happiness, #motivation to #bekind, and #positivevibes.

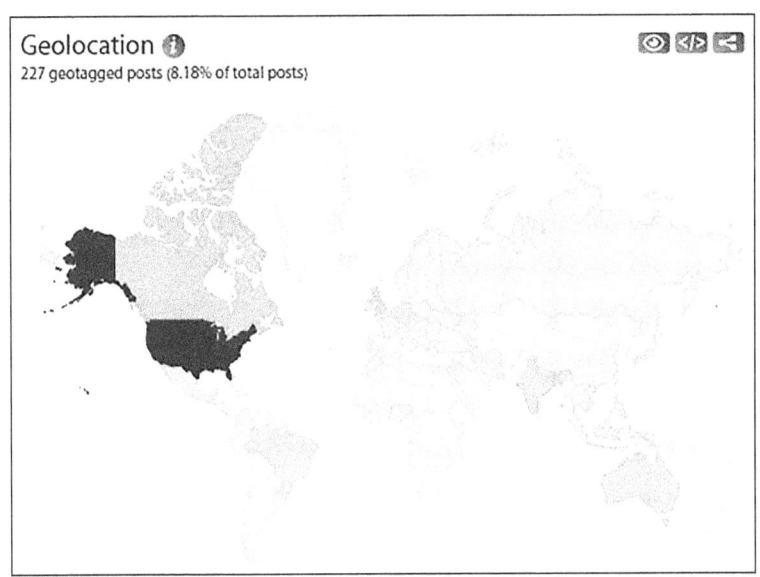

8.18% of post were geotagged. The 10 countries with most of the posts were the US (109), Canada (18), the UK (16),

Spirituality in the Selfie Culture of Instagram

India (13), Australia (9), Germany (7), France (7), Brazil (6), Italy (5), and Belarus (5). 2 posts from Ireland were also shown.

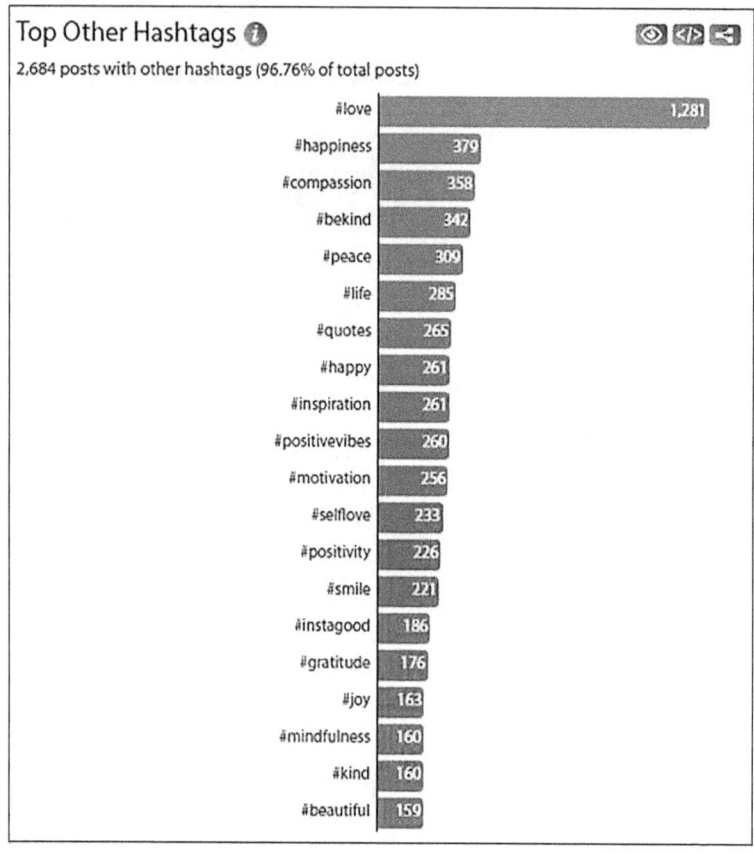

96.76 percent of posts used other hashtags, linking #kindness with #love, #happiness, and #compassion.

Kindness is inseparable from love, life, people, positivity, and compassion—all of which makes it a spiritual value—faith and soul are being mentioned as well. The emerging spiritual practice with kindness is mindfulness

Spirituality on Instagram

and it goes together with showing gratitude, building peace, feeling self-love and happiness, and expressing joy.

#LIVEAUTHENTIC

Spirituality in the Selfie Culture of Instagram

More than 14 million people have seen 2,880 posts with #liveauthentic which were displayed for 14.5 million times. They got 7,812 comments and 180,087 likes.

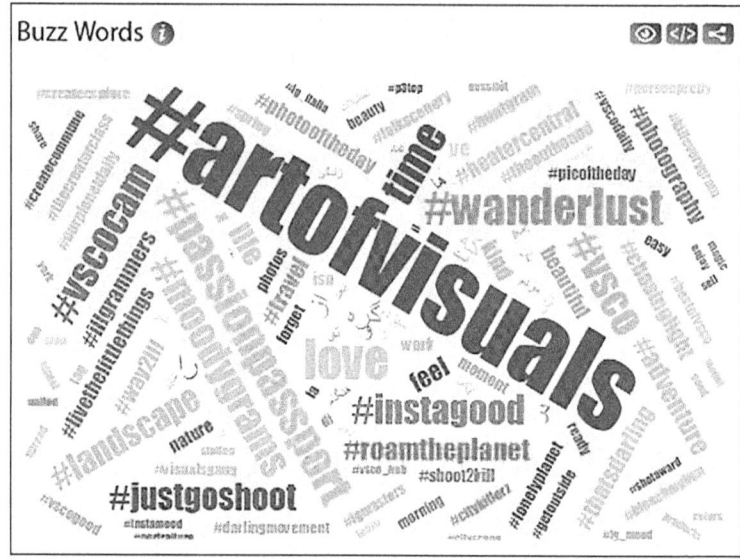

Buzzwords about #liveauthentic relate to #photography, #adventures in #nature, and #travel.

Spirituality on Instagram

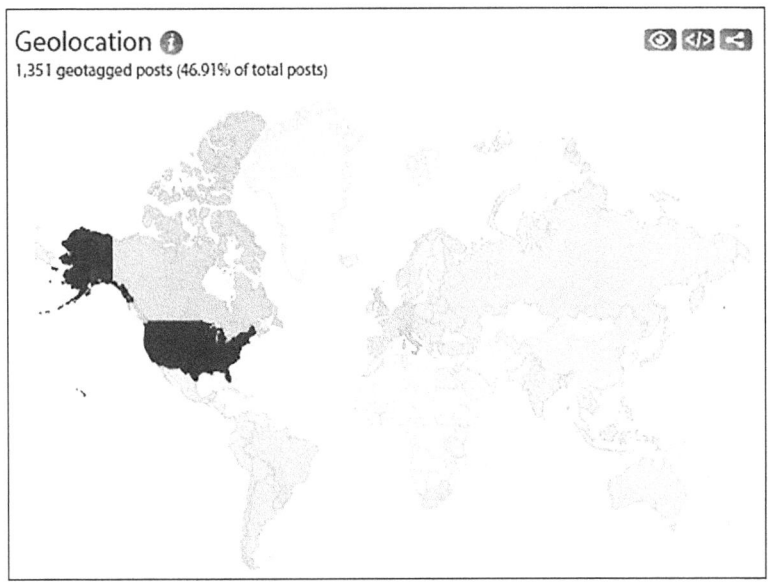

A high percentage of posts (46.91 percent) showed the location—again because of people posting while travelling. The 10 countries with most of the posts were the US (514), Italy (108), Canada (66), the UK (63), Germany (61), France (41), Indonesia (31), India (29), Spain (28), and Vietnam (27). There were 3 posts from Ireland.

Top Other Hashtags

2,550 posts with other hashtags (88.54% of total posts)

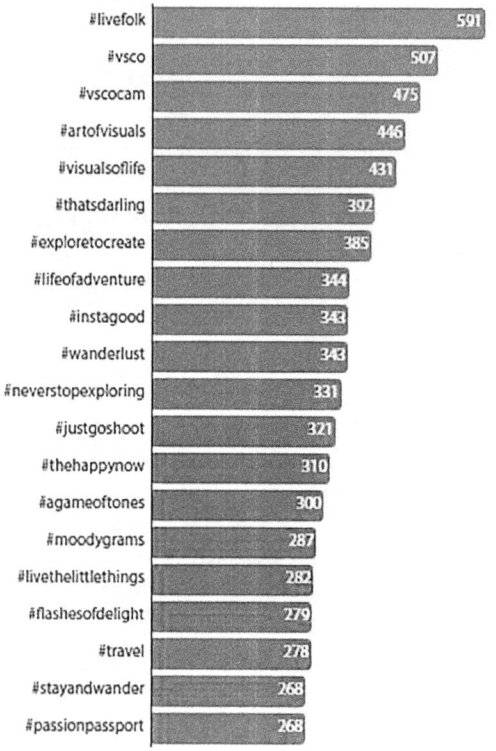

88.54 percent of posts had additional hashtags, mostly linked with travelling and photography.

#Liveauthentic is a hashtag people use when posting about authenticity in life (hashtag #authentic is linked with real or fake products/designs). From all the monitored hashtags, #liveauthentic got the most comments and likes—showing real engagement and impact on other Instagram users. The emerging spiritual themes are mostly travel and photography—creative ways to experience life and express one's emotions and feelings in the moment, shown by the

Spirituality on Instagram

hashtags #exploretocreate, #visualsoflife, #neverstopexploring, #livethelittlethings, and #thehappynow. There is no mention of spirituality in particular, but it is sometimes present in a form of secular spirituality.

The aim of this research was to investigate the occurrence of posts about spirituality on Instagram and the data gathered through the observed period, even for three days only, has shown that there is a big number of people all over the world who do post about spirituality on Instagram.

Spirituality in the Selfie Culture of Instagram

Hashtag	No. users	No. posts general	Top countries	No. posts Ireland	Top 3 linked terms	Emerging themes with Spirituality
#spirituality	2145	2884	USA, UK, India	0	spiritual, meditation, love	Wisdom, Inspiration, Enlightenment, Consciousness
#God	2588	3245	USA, Brazil, India	2	love, Jesus, faith	Prayer, Music, Art
#pray	1838	2505	USA, India, Canada	1	God, love, faith	Religion (Christianity, Islam), Sacred Books
#meditation	4077	4804	USA, UK, Canada	2	yoga, love, spirituality	Nature, Personal, Travel
#blessed	2704	3015	USA, Australia, Brazil	3	love, happy, grateful	Work, Family, Female
#grateful	2464	2679	USA, UK, Canada	2	blessed, love, thankful	Nature, Family, Friends
#truth	2967	3460	USA, Canada, UK	0	love, life, quotes	Faith, God, Bible
#love	2332	2518	USA, Italy, Brazil	0	instagood, photooftheday, likeforlike	Art, Travel, Family
#kindness	2285	2774	USA, Canada, UK	2	love, happiness, compassion	Mindfulness
#liveauthentic	2668	2880	USA, Italy, Canada	3	livefolk, vsco, artofvisuals	Travel, Photography

Spirituality on Instagram

According to the Instagram report for 2017, the 10 most used hashtags were:

1. #love
2. #fashion
3. #photooftheday
4. #photography
5. #art
6. #beautiful
7. #travel
8. #happy
9. #nature
10. #picoftheday[4]

Generally, this shows a positive nature of Instagram as a social media platform. The number of hashtags about spirituality, sometimes also connected with other most used hashtags, is a sign that Instagram is a very interesting medium for future, more detailed research. There was never such a great opportunity for researchers to take a look into so many personal stories and examples.

---

4. Instagram, "Instagram's 2017 Year in Review."

4

Future Challenges for Cyberspirituality

I AM AWARE THAT this study was limited by the amount of accessible data—there was no data about the age or other personal specifications of users, for example. That is due to the software used to obtain the data and the limitations to getting the data directly from Instagram. Another researcher might in the future use a different type of software, or a combination of multiple ones to get more details. Analyzing big data is very important for the future of academic research but there is a need for additional training in IT data analysis for researchers without this background.

It is important to bear in mind that this was an explorative study. There was no previous research of this type to refer to while designing this study. The results could be different if the analysis included a different set of hashtags, more connected to a specific religion or spiritual practices. However, the chosen set of hashtags has indicated the new types of spirituality emerging on the Internet. Social

Future Challenges for Cyberspirituality

networks are the channels for communication among individuals but also between individuals and institutions/communities. People do use them to communicate about everything, including spirituality. Also, this study concentrated on examining hashtags in English, and therefore it is not a complete record of all users that were posting about spirituality, as other languages were not considered.

The findings offer support for the premise that cyberspirituality should be defined as a separate research field about specific practices of expressing spiritual values on the Internet in the way described by David Perrin—a research about how the spiritual self is lived out. Spiritual framework of authentic subjectivity has proved to be a good way of looking into spiritual practices on Instagram. There is a sense of exploration and identification embedded in the process of posting on social media: you are editing, refining, and understanding yourself through the photographic journey in a search for beauty, truth, goodness, and love. It is therefore important to engage in further research of cyberspirituality, separate from digital religion or cybertheology.

The research confirmed that most of the posts about spirituality on Instagram belongs to the category of secular spirituality. This was one of the expected findings. Mindfulness, yoga, meditation—all these spiritual practices were present in a significant number of posts. Spirituality expressed in them is often deeply personal, a way of presenting to the world one's true self. It is horizontal, not looking for the authority or approval from a traditional religious community—it seeks communication and connectedness with similar people, the ones who share the same quest and journey towards the sacred. Visually, many photos from this category are taken in nature, in places not necessarily considered as sacred by any religious criteria.

Spirituality in the Selfie Culture of Instagram

There were also many examples of people using Instagram to share about their religious tradition, especially Christianity and Islam, by using the hashtags #God and #pray. Both sacred books—the Bible and the Quran—were used to find an inspiration. These kinds of posts would belong more into the category of digital religion than cyberspirituality.

One of the interesting findings in this discourse is the presence of art as a medium to communicate about spirituality on Instagram. Photography is not only the tool used to create the published content but very often presents a moment of stillness or meditation. One needs to stop, to concentrate, and to notice things before capturing a good photo—it calls for being in the moment. It may capture a feeling, an inspiration, an inner vision, a path—it is used as a journaling entry on a spiritual journey, sometimes shared only with personal intention to keep it as a memory and sometimes as a tool for communication. Photographing and sharing a life journey can help to bring spirituality into everyday moments and create a spiritual narrative of one's personal story.

Photography as a spiritual practice is well recognized in the works of Thomas Merton. Merton pointed out that, "as we go about the world, everything we meet and everything we see and hear and touch, far from defiling, purifies and plants in us something more of contemplation and of heaven."[1] He believed that his passion for photography was enabling what he called "the urgency of seeing, fully aware, experiencing what is here."[2] Merton held an opinion that a camera can help us to raise awareness about the moment, to see things differently, and to create something new. He made a difference between his regular photographic work,

1. Merton, *Seeds of Contemplation*, 22.
2. Merton, *Turning Toward the World*, 123.

showing events, places, and people, and his photos done as an experience of meditation. Merton's photography reflected his contemplative vision and practices, showing that photography and contemplation can go hand in hand.

If we can talk about "selfie culture" on social media, we can also say that sometimes we see "selfie spirituality" as well. Posting on social media is the individual's way of advertising themselves and their lifestyle. Sacred acts or worship are no exception to the self-documentation craze. In the context of individualism expressed on social media and lack of traditional communities, spirituality can also become a passing trend, a new cultural addiction, or a well-paid business. All these traps are often not only supported but sometimes also misused by consumer culture and corporate marketing strategies.

Social media can also evoke a higher degree of polarization in our societies. We encounter the endless number of people with different or opposing opinions and sets of values. If we don't want to communicate with them, we can easily "block" them and close ourselves inside the digital bubbles where we are surrounded only with voices who flatter us and agree with us, which can lead to a higher sense of righteousness. Some social media platforms even encourage such scenarios by running constant (imposed or self-learning) algorithms that filter out content and opinions that differ with the individual user's opinions and mindsets, leading them to believe that everybody around them has the same beliefs, horizons, or sense for aesthetics.

There is no doubt that social media, if used too much or is being misused, can have negative impacts on individuals and societies. It is based on the engagement business model—more users produce more content, the number of views rises and there is lots of activity which can then be analyzed and sold to the advertisers. One of the problems is that negative emotions trigger many more reactions and activity than the positive ones. The majority of platforms don't really care about the quality or truthfulness of the content, whether or not the videos are real, whether or not the conspiracy theories are true, or whether disturbing content is aimed at children—which is harmful for society. Tech industry is becoming the largest political actor in the world, influencing a billion people's attention, thoughts, and decisions every day. Fake news, misinformation, snd mistruth are the words we hear more and more in relation to social media giants.

Additionally, technology has addictive qualities that need to be addressed. Internet Addiction Disorder seems to affect the pleasure center of the brain. The addictive behavior triggers a release of dopamine to promote the pleasurable experience. Over time, more and more of the activity is needed to induce the same pleasurable response, creating a dependency. The theory of Internet Addiction Disorder is that digital technology users experience multiple layers of reward when they use various applications. Online activities (surfing, pornography, chat rooms, message boards, social media, video games, email, texting, cloud applications, and games, etc.) may support so-called reward experiences, for example pornography (sexual stimulation), video games (identification with a hero, immersive graphics), dating sites (romantic fantasy), online poker (financial desires), and special interest chat rooms or message boards (sense of belonging). As with other addictions, when activated, dopamine release is increased.[3] Internet addiction is not included in the latest *Diagnostic and Statistical Manual of Mental Disorders* by the American Psychiatric Association, but there is an ongoing research looking into the effect on human behavior.

---

3. Cash et al, "Internet Addiction," 292–98.

Future Challenges for Cyberspirituality

However, that doesn't mean that all of us should stop using the Internet and social media completely. Digital natives do not know life without the Internet and social media, and these things are a crucial part of their identity. Just like televangelism or expressing spirituality through traditional media, a selfie from a pilgrimage can be an uplifting message to thousands of people throughout the globe, an act of kindness can inspire people to do the same in their local settings, a social injustice can produce a motivation to search for a new authority. Sandra Schneiders writes that "Today we recognize that the subject of Christian spirituality is the human being as a whole; spirit, mind and body; individual and social; culturally conditioned and ecologically intertwined with all creation; economically and politically responsible."[4] Spirituality in general, not only Christian spirituality, cannot be lived without having a connection and relationship with the world, with concrete realities and circumstances in which people live. Social media is therefore an important channel not only for individuals but for different spiritual groups or practices as well.

Considering the number of Instagram users in Ireland—over 600,000 adults aged 15+ use Instagram on a daily basis[5]—it was surprising that there were almost no posts found from the Republic. There is a possibility that users from Ireland are posting more but not tagging their location in the posts or that the research could not grab the data because the users have private (locked) profiles. The low number of posts also indicates that the institutions providing spiritual services—churches, religious communities, retreat houses, etc.—are not using Instagram as a communication channel. Another possible conclusion coming from the findings is that young generations in Ireland, who

4. Schneiders, "Approaches to the Study of Christian Spirituality," 17.
5. Porter, "Social Networking—Nov 17."

are the main users of Instagram, either have no interest in spirituality or feel uncomfortable talking about it on the Internet.

The post-secular context in which young generations live today presents new opportunities for building spiritual capital, with social media as one of the tools. There is a chance to share spirituality with people who are no longer going to church, with ones who describe themselves as "spiritual but not religious" as well as with people belonging to different religious backgrounds. Social media can be helpful in recreating and reclaiming a spiritual narrative, separately from traditional media. According to Instagram, 75 percent of users act after being inspired by a post, like visiting a website, searching, shopping, or telling a friend.[6] Using this platform to post about spirituality or to offer different services—such as retreats, pilgrimages, spiritual accompaniment, etc.—would be a great way to reach many people. Using social media, especially Instagram and Snapchat, is the main way to communicate with young generations today, as they perceive them as a part of their identity. Sharing personal stories, talking about community life, and offering guidance and help on the Internet can be a good strategy for vocational directors who are trying to promote religious life in their congregations.

Communication is a key concept in social media in general. For example, social media pages belonging to organizations, businesses, or celebrities (including religious leaders) will be more visible (or receive more reach) when they provide and contain more interactions (such as likes, comments, and options to ask and receive answers). One of the mistakes often made by people or institutions who run these pages is that they view them only as a board, a static place where they can publish something and impose

6. Instagram For Business, "Hitting 500,000 Advertisers."

Future Challenges for Cyberspirituality

information upon their followers. Another very important aspect is authenticity. Ignoring the feedback from other users will result in them losing interest and breaking the communication. The Internet, and social media, have brought the democratization of knowledge and democratization of communication—anyone can have a voice and everyone's voice is equal. The only way that someone's voice will be heard and appreciated lies in the level of their authenticity online, not in the role or position they hold in real life.

Some areas for further research therefore might be an attempt to derive important spirituality themes, or those which were shared by influential Instagram users, especially those with a religious background, and to take a deeper look into the frequency and quality of social media use among the religious institutions in Ireland. A similar study like this one could be conducted using additional data such as age information to better identify the demographics and narratives in different parts of the world. This would allow researchers to explore whether specific generations have different types of spirituality and what their needs are. Data from several different languages could help to build a better picture about the current cyberspirituality trends. Further research could also include exploration of photojournaling as a spiritual practice, the importance of social media presence and activity for vocational purposes, and offering spiritual accompaniment services online.

This research might help to improve some areas of current practice in use of social media among spiritual directors, retreat houses, religious orders, and individuals. The number of posts about spirituality on Instagram is an indicator that, to either talk about it or advocate certain spiritual practices, social media is a tool that needs to be used for communication with others. Although this research looked only into Instagram, the same applies to other social media apps as well as the websites. It would be important to engage in developing digital skills among individuals who are offering services in the field of spirituality through social media trainings, for example. The institutions could think about developing digital strategies and creating better content management by employing media professionals.

To conclude, the study generated important data in relation to cyberspirituality and showed the need for further development and research in this field. It also showed that there is a lot of opportunity for individuals and communities to develop spiritual narrative in communicating on line, especially with young people who are more likely to express themselves as "spiritual but not religious." Spiritual authenticity on social media as a part of building spiritual capital is an important step.

Glossary

Application (App): A mobile application, most commonly referred to as an app, is a type of software designed to run on a mobile device such as a smartphone or tablet computer.

Avatar: An avatar is a computer-generated three-dimensional image representing someone in a virtual environment. It may be a two-dimensional image or a moving three-dimensional figure.

Big Data: Big data are extremely large data sets that may be analysed by computers to reveal patterns, trends and associations, especially relating to human behaviour and interactions.

Blog: Short for "web log" or "weblog," a blog was originally a type of online diary in the form of a website owned and created by an individual.

Buzzword: A buzzword is a word or phrase that is fashionable at a particular time or in a particular context.

Computer Algorithms: Computer algorithms are well-defined procedures that allow a computer to solve a problem.

Glossary

A particular problem can typically be solved by more than one algorithm. Optimization is the process of finding the most efficient algorithm for a given task.

Cyberchurch: Cyberchurch refers to a wide variety of ways using the Internet by religious groups to facilitate its activities, particularly worship services.

Cyberculture: Cyberculture refers to the distinctive identity formations and community constructions enabled by digitally networked technologies.

Cyberspace: Cyberspace is a nonphysical environment that enables individuals to interact with other individuals or with sets of information via digital connections.

Digital Media: Digital media is any type of electronic media that is based on binary code. Examples include the web, video games, digital audio, or video and artwork created using computer software.

Digital Native: A digital native is a person born or brought up during the age of digital technology, familiar with computers and the Internet from an early age.

Facebook: Facebook is a social media network that allows users to create profiles, upload photos and video, send messages, organize in groups, and communicate with others.

Facebook/Instagram page: A public profile created by businesses, organizations or celebrities, a Facebook or Instagram page works much like a personal profile, except that they have "followers" instead of "friends."

Glossary

Geotagging: Geotagging is the process of adding geographical identification metadata to various media, such as photo or video.

Hashtag: A word or phrase with a hash sign (#), a hashtag is used on social media to categorize and identify messages on a specific topic.

Internet: The Internet is a global computer network providing a variety of information and communication facilities, consisting of interconnected networks using standardized communication protocols.

Impressions: Impressions are the number of times someone's content is displayed, no matter if it was clicked or not.

Reach: Reach is the total number of people who see someone's content.

Selfie: A selfie is a self-portrait photo, usually shared on social media.

Smartphone: A smartsphone is a mobile phone that performs many of the functions of a computer, typically having a touch screen interface, Internet access, and an operating system capable of running downloaded apps.

Tags: Tags are keywords used to classify content.

Twitter: Twitter is an online social media network for sharing information in text messages of 140 characters or fewer.

Glossary

Virtual World: A virtual world is a nonphysical, digitally created environment in which one or more users or players can interact.

Web 1.0: Web 1.0 was the first stage in the World Wide Web, which was entirely made up of static web pages, not yet providing interactive content.

Web 2.0: Web 2.0 is the intersection of web application features that not only delivers static images and text but also facilitates user interactivity (social networking, tagging, collaborative authoring, media distribution, and keyword searches).

YouTube: YouTube is an online social media video-sharing site. It allows users to upload short videos for others to view.

Bibliography

Balakrishnan, Janarthanan, and Mark D. Griffiths. "An Exploratory Study of "Selfitis" and the Development of the Selfitis Behavior Scale." *International Journal of Mental Health and Addiction* 16 (2017) 722–36.

Benedict XVI. "Social Networks: portals of truth and faith; new spaces for evangelization." http://w2.vatican.va/content/benedict-xvi/en/messages/communications/documents/hf_ben-xvi_mes_20130124_47th-world-communications-day.html.

Campbell, Heidi A., and Vitullo Alessandra. "Assessing Changes in the Study of Religious Communities in Digital Religion Studies." *Church, Communication and Culture* 1 (2016) 73–89.

Campbell, Heidi A. *Digital Religion: Understanding Religious Practice in New Media Worlds*. New York: Routledge, 2013.

———. "Spiritualising the Internet: Uncovering Discourse and Narrative of Religious Internet Usage." *Heidelberg Journal of Religions on the Internet* 1 (2005) 1–26.

Cash, Hilarie, et al. "Internet Addiction: A Brief Summary of Research and Practice." *Current Psychiatry Reviews* 8 (2012) 292–98.

Cobb, Jennifer. *CyberGrace: the Search for God in the Digital World*. New York: Crown, 1998.

Díez Bosch, Míriam, et al. "Typing My Religion: Digital Use of Religious Webs and Apps by Adolescents and Youth for Religious and Interreligious Dialogue." *Church, Communication and Culture* 2 (2017) 121–43.

Drescher, Elizabeth. *Tweet If You Heart Jesus: Practicing Church in the Digital Reformation*. Harrisburg, PA: Morehouse, 2011.

Finnegan, Jack. *The Audacity of Spirit: the Meaning and Shaping of Spirituality Today*. Dublin: Veritas, 2008.

Bibliography

Friedman, Thomas L. *The Lexus And the Olive Tree: Understanding Globalization.* New York: Anchor, 2000.

Galuppo, Maria Mercedes. "Millennials Are Expected to Take a Massive Number of Selfies in Their Lifetimes." https://www.aol.com/article/news/2017/05/19/millennials-expected-to-take-over-25-000-selfies-in-their-lifeti/22099995/?guccounter=1.

Groeschel, Craig. *#Struggles: Following Jesus in a Selfie-Centered World.* Grand Rapids: Zondervan, 2015.

Guzek, Damian. "Discovering the Digital Authority: Twitter as Reporting Tool for Papal Activities." *Heidelberg Journal of Religions on the Internet* 9 (2015) 63–80.

Helland, Christopher. "Online-Religion/Religion-Online and Virtual Communitas." In *Religion on The Internet: Research Prospects and Promises* edited by Douglas E. Cowan and Jeffrey K. Hadden, 205–223. New York: JAI, 2000.

Helland, Christopher. "Popular Religion and the World Wide Web: a Match Made in (Cyber) Heaven". In *Religion Online: Finding Faith on The Internet*, edited by L.L. Dawson and D.E. Cowan, 21–33. New York: Routledge, 2004.

Huges Rinker, Cortney, et al. "Religious Apps for Smartphones and Tablets: Transforming Religious Authority and The Nature of Religion." *Interdisciplinary Journal of Research on Religion* 12 (2016) 1–14.

Instagram. "Instagram's 2017 Year in Review." https://instagram-press.com/blog/2017/11/29/instagrams-2017-year-in-review/.

Instagram for Business. "Hitting 500,000 Advertisers." https://business.instagram.com/blog/500000-advertisers/.

Jonveaux, Isabelle. "Facebook as a Monastic Place? The New Use of Internet by Catholic Monks". *ScriptaInstitutiDonnerianiAboensis* 25 (2013) 99–109.

Lipka, Michael. "Millennials Increasingly are Driving Growth of 'Nones.'" *Pew Research Center* (2015). http://www.pewresearch.org/fact-tank/2015/05/12/millennials-increasingly-are-driving-growth-of-nones/.

Lipka, Michael, and Claire Gecewicz. "More Americans Now Say They're Spiritual but Not Religious." *Pew Research Center* (2017). http://www.pewresearch.org/fact-tank/2017/09/06/more-americans-now-say-theyre-spiritual-but-not-religious/.

Lister, Mary. "33 Mind-Boggling Instagram Stats & Facts For 2018." *Wordstream* (2017). https://www.wordstream.com/blog/ws/2017/04/20/instagram-statistics.

Bibliography

Masci, David, and Conrad Hackett. "Meditation Is Common Across Many Religious Groups in the U.S." *Pew Research Center* (2018). http://www.pewresearch.org/fact-tank/2018/01/02/meditation-is-common-across-many-religious-groups-in-the-u-s/.

McGarry, Patsy. "Young Irish People Among the Most Religious In Europe." *The Irish Times* (2018). https://www.irishtimes.com/news/social-affairs/religion-and-beliefs/young-irish-people-among-the-most-religious-in-europe-1.3441046.

Mercadante, Linda A. *Belief Without Borders: Inside the Minds of the Spiritual but Not Religious*. New York: Oxford University Press, 2014.

———. "Understanding the Spiritual but Not Religious." https://www.uua.org/sites/live-new.uua.org/files/spiritual_not_religious.pdf, 2018.

Merton, Thomas. *Seeds of Contemplation*. New York: New Directions, 1949.

———. *Turning Toward the World: the Pivotal Years*. San Francisco: Harper Collins, 1996.

Miller, Vincent. *Understanding Digital Culture*. Thousand Oaks: Sage, 2011.

Molina, Noelia. *Religious Vocations in Ireland: Challenges and Opportunities*. Dublin: Vocations Ireland, 2017.

Moore, Thomas. "A Religion of One's Own." http://thomasmooresoul.com/a-religion-of-ones-own/.

Newman, Jay. *Religion and Technology: A Study In The Philosophy Of Culture*. Santa Barbara: Praeger, 1997.

Norton, Belinda, and Rebecca Porter. "Social Networking—Aug 2017." *Ipsos* (2018). https://www.ipsos.com/en-ie/social-networking-aug-2017.

O'Sullivan, Michael. "Authenticity as a Spiritual Process." Lecture, WIT Moodle, 2017.

———. "Reflexive and Transformative Subjectivity: Authentic Spirituality and a Journey with Incest." In *Sources of Transformation: Revitalizing Christian Spirituality*, edited by Edward Howells, 173–82. London: Continuum, 2010.

Perrin, David B. *Studying Christian Spirituality*. New York: Routledge, 2007.

Porter, Rebecca. "Social Networking—Nov 17." *Ipsos* (2018). https://www.ipsos.com/en-ie/social-networking-nov-17.

Rose, Gillian. *Visual Methodologies: An Introduction to the Interpretation of Visual Materials*. London: Sage, 2001.

Bibliography

Rutledge, Pamela. "#Selfies: Narcissism or Self-Exploration?" *Psychology Today* (2013). http://www.psychologytoday.com/blog/positively-media/201304/selfies narcissism-or-self-exploration.

Schneiders, Sandra. "Approaches to the Study of Christian Spirituality." In *The Blackwell Companion to Christian Spirituality*, edited by Arthur Holder, 15–33. Oxford: Blackwell, 2005.

Sheldrake, Philip. *Spirituality—a Guide for the Perplexed*. London: Bloomsbury Academic, 2014.

Spadaro, Antonio. *Cybertheology*. New York: Fordham University Press, 2014.

Storr, Will. *Selfie*. London: Picador, 2017.

Sweet, Leonard. *Viral: How Social Networking is Poised to Ignite Revival*. Colorado Springs: WaterBrook, 2012.

Tobin, Ronan B. "A Hitchhiker's Guide to Cyberspirituality." *The Furrow* 55 (2004) 591–97.

Tomeo, Theresa. *Beyond Me, My Selfie & I: Finding Real Happiness in a Self-Absorbed World*. Cincinnati: Servant, 2016.

Turkle, Sherry. *Life on the Screen: Identity in the Age of the Internet*. New York: Touchstone, 1995.

Twenge, Jean M., and W. Keith Campbell. *The Narcissism Epidemic: Living in the Age of Entitlement*. New York: Atria, 2009.

Van Ness, Peter H. *Spirituality and the Secular Quest*. New York: Crossroad, 1996.

Yu, Gino, and Michael Highland. "Communicating Spiritual Experience with Video Game Technology." *Heidelberg Journal of Religions on the Internet* 31 (2008) 267–89.

Zirdejveld, Theo. "Pope Francis In Cairo: Authority and Branding on Instagram." *Heidelberg Journal of Religions on the Internet* 12 (2017) 125–40.

www.ingramcontent.com/pod-product-compliance
Lightning Source LLC
Chambersburg PA
CBHW070511090426
42735CB00012B/2742